Cambridge Elements ≡

Elements in Shakespeare Performance
edited by
W. B. Worthen
Barnard College

APPROACHING THE INTERVAL IN THE EARLY MODERN THEATRE

The Significance of the 'Act-Time'

Mark Hutchings
University of Salamanca

CAMBRIDGE
UNIVERSITY PRESS

Shaftesbury Road, Cambridge CB2 8EA, United Kingdom

One Liberty Plaza, 20th Floor, New York, NY 10006, USA

477 Williamstown Road, Port Melbourne, VIC 3207, Australia

314–321, 3rd Floor, Plot 3, Splendor Forum, Jasola District Centre,
New Delhi – 110025, India

103 Penang Road, #05–06/07, Visioncrest Commercial, Singapore 238467

Cambridge University Press is part of Cambridge University Press & Assessment,
a department of the University of Cambridge.

We share the University's mission to contribute to society through the pursuit of
education, learning and research at the highest international levels of excellence.

www.cambridge.org
Information on this title: www.cambridge.org/9781108791922

DOI: 10.1017/9781108866842

First published 2024

A catalogue record for this publication is available from the British Library.

ISBN 978-1-108-79192-2 Paperback
ISSN 2516-0117 (online)
ISSN 2516-0109 (print)

Approaching the Interval in the Early Modern Theatre
The Significance of the 'Act-Time'

Elements in Shakespeare Performance

DOI: 10.1017/9781108866842
First published online: March 2024

Mark Hutchings
University of Salamanca

Author for correspondence: Mark Hutchings, Mark.Hutchings@usal.es
m.p.v.hutchings@reading.ac.uk

ABSTRACT: In requiring artificial light, the early modern indoor theatre had to interrupt the action so that the candles could be attended to, if necessary. The origin of the five-act, four-interval play was not classical drama but candle technology. This Element explores the implications of this aspect of playmaking. Drawing on evidence in surviving texts it explores how the interval affected composition and stagecraft, how it provided opportunities for stage-sitters, and how amphitheatre plays were converted for indoor performance (and vice versa). Recovering the interval yields new insights into familiar texts and brings into the foreground interesting examples of how the interval functioned in lesser-known plays. This Element concludes with a discussion of how this aspect of theatre might feed into the debate over the King's Men's repertory management in its Globe-Blackfriars years and sets out the wider implications for both the modern theatre and the academy.

KEYWORDS: act-division, candlelight, interval, stagecraft, stage-sitting

ISBNs: 9781108791922 (PB), 9781108866842 (OC)
ISSNs: 2516-0117 (online), 2516-0109 (print)

Contents

1 Introduction   1

2 Candles and Questions   10

3 Scripting the 'Act-Time'   25

4 Amphitheatre < > Hall   40

5 The Globe < > Blackfriars Effect   53

6 Coda   69

   Appendix   79

   References   92

1 Introduction

It might seem counterintuitive to consider the theatre interval worthy of examination. After all, in modern performance a scheduled interruption tends to function as little more than a pause in the action, usually signalling the passing of time and often facilitating a change of set, the stage darkened or curtained; meanwhile, the audience take refreshment or 'comfort breaks', the sale of alcohol often an important factor in a production's financial viability. On the page it is barely noticeable, rendered opaque as white space between the acts, a Melvillesque visible absence of drama. But as familiar to the theatregoer and of practical import to directors though it is – as the rich history of Shakespeare in modern revival attests (Holland 2001) – the interval is simultaneously incorporated and erased, with seemingly limited scope for critical engagement. As this Element will show, however, in the early modern theatre the interval had a profound influence on the design, performance, and experience of drama. The 'act-time', as early moderns knew it, invites us not only to consider afresh how we navigate the earliest textual witnesses but also rethink some of the assumptions underpinning modern editorial practices. The principal aim of this Element, therefore, is to recuperate the interval and urge its reintegration into our understanding of theatre-making in this period.

Not only popularly, through films such as Olivier's *Henry V* (1944) and the Shakespeare's Globe project, but also to a considerable degree in the academy, the 16th-/17th-century theatre is principally defined by the iconic amphitheatre. The 'romance of the open-air theaters' (Cohen 2009, 209) is at the heart of a narrative we construct that tends to relegate the less exotic indoor space to a subordinate role. Consequentially, a tendency (conscious or otherwise) to regard the outdoor playhouse as the default performance model has obscured distinctive practices indoors – which, on tour, were the norm, not the exception (Somerset 1994). Thus, situating plays with established indoor provenance in their appropriate context brings to light characteristics otherwise unseen – *unseeable*, even – which has important implications for performance studies and editorial practices distorted by assumptions grounded in amphitheatre-centred modelling.

To be sure, this situation is changing. The still-authoritative account of the best-known of these venues, the Blackfriars playhouse (Smith 1964), has been augmented in recent years by a number of studies, each directing attention to the indoor playhouse (Menzer 2006; Cohen 2009; Gurr and Karim-Cooper 2014; Dustagheer 2017; Tosh 2018; Munro 2020). Thanks to the long-established, multi-volume *Records of Early English Drama* (REED) the extent of indoor playmaking across the land has now been comprehensively mapped, this scholarship taking in guildhalls, grand houses, the universities, and the Inns of Court; similarly, theatricals in the royal palaces have been revisited (Astington 1999; Dutton 2016; Streitberger 2016). Another sign of this rebalancing is the opening of two 'replica' indoor spaces with the aim of experimenting with 'original practices' (OPs) – the American Shakespeare Center (ASC) Blackfriars in Staunton, Virginia, in 2001, and the Sam Wanamaker Playhouse (SWP), a subdivision of Shakespeare's Globe in London – both of which have drawn on and fed into scholarly research. While the ASC is a conjectural 'reconstruction' of the (remodelled, second) Blackfriars, its London counterpart's claim to represent an indoor 'archetype' has left it open to criticism (Syme 2018); nevertheless, the SWP has been particularly influential in shaping recent academic discourse, most of the recent cluster of studies cited earlier being directly or indirectly linked with the theatre since it opened in 2014.

It is true that theatre historians have long understood that the open-to-the-skies, 'public' amphitheatres, located in the liberties, differed in important respects from the roofed, 'private' hall playhouses, situated within the city walls, though the binary framing obscures some differences in of design (insofar as this information is retrievable) and (probably) practices within each category. That notwithstanding, the nature and significance of those differences – in terms of size, audience capacity and demographic, theatre design and stage space, acting style, theatre machinery, musical and acoustical accompaniment, and repertory management – has been much debated. On the one hand, that adult companies were accustomed to alternating between, say, a London amphitheatre and an indoor space (on tour, at court), points to flexibility; on the other hand, children's troupes always performed indoors, and developed specific attributes arising from those circumstances that emphasized difference rather than continuity across formats. Yet static models cannot account for the passage of time, cross-fertilization, and innovations in stagecraft. To take one prominent example, what did the King's Men do when they were able finally to run an indoor theatre in tandem with their amphitheatre? The short answer is: we do not know. But adjustments to their repertory management there must have been. One view, emphasizing difference, has it that the company effectively ran separate repertories. Thus, logically, the old, outdoor plays – practically the whole of the Shakespeare canon – remained at the amphitheatre (for which they were originally designed), while the new plays were moulded to the conditions at the Blackfriars (Bentley 1948). Alternatively, and for which there is an emerging consensus, a more flexible, dual-playhouse model was developed, which allowed for inter-theatre movement. Correspondingly (and necessarily), some of the established markers of difference, such as audience composition (and therefore taste, with implications for matters such as genre and repertory), have been challenged, easing the path towards a model that, after all, makes economic sense (Knutson 2006, 59). This argument, as will become clear, touches centrally on whether, therefore, at some point in the early 17th century, indoor and outdoor practices converged – not only locally, for the King's Men, but across the board (see Taylor 1993).

To arrive at such a juncture, however, requires a significant readjustment in how theatre historians tell the story of drama in early modern England. Curiously, the most striking mark of difference between the two traditions, the indoor practice of interrupting the action at points in the performance, has been virtually ignored. Recent studies devoted to children's companies (e.g. Bly 2000; Munro 2005) are entirely silent on the matter. At best scholars allude to it *en passant*, presumably on the assumption that there is nothing more to say beyond dutiful acknowledgment (where this happens), or that, as with the modern *intermission*, the interval is not understood as part of the play at all – for either playgoer or playreader. Crucially, it is not considered to be a factor in a play's design, though curiously the modern practice of dividing productions of early modern plays into two or more parts *is*. These decisions give the play-narrative a particular shape, though *not* as originally conceived: Peter Holland rightly challenges Emrys Jones's view that Shakespeare deliberately structured his plays as two halves pivoting on a single act-break (Jones 1971, 66–88), pointing out that this is to impose modern practices on those of centuries ago (Holland 2001, 129). This goes to the heart of the matter. To understand the function and significance of the early modern interval requires that we decouple it from its modern successor and historicize it as a distinctively early modern phenomenon.

1.1 Backstory

Thomas Kuhn famously contended that evidence does not speak for itself but is interpreted through and according to a scholarly consensus, or paradigm (Kuhn 1996). Evidence- and experiment-based research, that is, is subject to sociological as well as scientific evaluation: findings presented to the scholarly community are deemed acceptable, or – if falling foul of the ruling paradigm – rejected. Only with the emergence of one or both of two conditions can this be challenged: 'novelties of fact' and 'novelties of theory' (Kuhn 1996, 52–65). In other words, discoveries or approaches that are so persuasive that the prevailing consensus is no longer tenable, necessitating its replacement. Kuhn's theory offers an incisive way of reading the history of Shakespearean textual scholarship (Mowat 2001, 18–26); this Element does not present 'novelties of fact' as such, but it does offer a new perspective on canonical and less familiar texts to challenge current thinking.

One of the puzzles that have bedevilled scholarship since the 18th century is the structural variation in printed drama, especially in the bibliographically rich and culturally central Shakespeare canon. How to explain the disparity in the First Folio, where some plays are divided and others not, and between the 1623 compendium and the previously published quartos: what might this disparity tell us, about the Shakespeare corpus and beyond? The issue is deemed less urgent today, but influenced by the earliest editors 20th-century scholars established a paradigm that would determine the scope of their investigation. Working as they were when drama was considered primarily in literary terms, they approached these texts with little concern for performance. Not illogically, in their desire to understand the problem scholars fixed on the Humanist recovery of Roman drama and its integration into the grammar school curriculum in the 16th century. T.W. Baldwin's weighty *William Shakspere's Five-Act Structure* (1947) and *On Act and Scene Division in the Shakspere First Folio* (1965),

Wilfred T. Jewkes's *Act Division in Elizabethan and Jacobean Plays* (1958), and Henry L. Snuggs's *Shakespeare and Five Acts* (1960) are all so constrained. Certainly, in the schoolroom boys who would become the first professional dramatists encountered the drama of Seneca, Plautus, and Terence divided into five acts, a format subsequently adopted for the printing of English plays in the 17th century and normalized by 18th-century editors of Shakespeare and their modern successors. But, unfortunately, this logic overdetermined the paradigm's parameters. Take this from Baldwin:

> Chapman, the classicist, would certainly have composed in acts, and his plays for the children's companies were uniformly so printed, but his two plays for the Admiral's were undivided in print, as were, at that time, most of the plays for that company and for all other companies of men. (Baldwin 1947, 65)

Here, in a single sentence, misled by a preoccupation with the (educated) author-figure ('the *classicist*'), Baldwin unwittingly identifies a key distinction between the practices of the children's and adult companies (and, crucially, theatres), but he is unable to pursue it – trapped by the ruling paradigm. 'Nor was it a matter of different theatres for men' (65): Baldwin *almost* stumbles on the critical difference between indoor and outdoor playmaking.

It is all too easy to identify error in the methodologies of previous generations of scholars. Within the paradigm it would have been illogical *not* to trace act-division back to Roman drama, for dramatists – and publishers and printers – were indeed so influenced. Unfortunately, however, it was based on a false genealogy. Ironically, Horace's five-act *theory* was precisely that, for 'the evidence indicates that continuous performance was the practice with Roman theatre' (Holland 2001, 137) – just as it would be in the English amphitheatres that evoked their 'ancestors'. Crucially, these scholars were looking in the wrong place. While it is understandable that they allowed what we would now call confirmation bias to rule out alternative explanations for the division or non-division of plays, the paradigm forced upon them a tortuous logic that typifies the New Bibliographers' faith in their method. While act-division sometimes reflected *compositional* preferences, it was theatre type that determined how a *performance* was structured. Philip Henslowe's records indicate that some plays were composed with a five-act structure in mind (Carson 1988, 56–9), rather than, more commonly, in scenes, but this presented scholars with a puzzle they ultimately failed to solve, wedded as they were to an author-centred approach that blinded them to other forms of agency, both in the theatre and in the printing house; where scholars should have discriminated, they conflated, 'fail[ing] to distinguish four separate aspects of the problem: acts and scenes in composition, in literary theory, in performance, and in the printing house' (Turner 2006, 178).

As is beginning to be understood, there is a simple reason for act-breaks in performance, for which the evidence (but not the paradigm) was always there. Whereas the purpose-built amphitheatres were open to the skies, benefitting from natural light, in the adapted indoor spaces the windows could not admit sufficient sunlight; thus, artificial light was needed as well – or, for performances held at night, instead. This was the case at court, and in any other indoor space in London or around the country. Crucially this raised a practical issue. Made of tallow (animal fat) or wax, candles could not last for the duration of a performance because the wicks required regular attention (Graves 1999, 14–15). This posed a practical problem. R.B. Graves suggests that a

> two- to three-hour performance in a hall theater lit by several dozen … inferior tallow candles could therefore require hundreds of individual snuffing operations, but only rarely do playwrights make provision for this necessity in their texts. (14)

In fact, as we shall see, *all* such texts make this provision. Ironically, the classical five-act structure did indeed provide a template for playmakers – only not as Baldwin et al. imagined; the four act-breaks provided an opportunity to check or mend the candles. This was so for amphitheatre-designed plays later adapted for indoor performance – where it became necessary to insert act-breaks – and for plays originally composed for staging with candlelight; in the case of the latter, this guided composition accordingly, but both processes involved the calculation of time (and therefore act-length). The humble candle, rather than an education in the classics, begot the interval.

1.2 Archive of Evidence

Absent the obstructive paradigm, these issues can be addressed afresh. The evidence trail is considerable. Court accounts; Henslowe's records; theatre designs and visual representations; manuscript plays; marked-up playbooks and printed texts; stage plots; accounts of playgoing; company scribe interventions; paratextual matter; printed plays; title-page attributions; playreaders' annotations; adapters' alterations: the interval has left many traces. Much of this material is familiar – not 'novelties of fact' at all. Exactly a century ago one of the foundational texts of modern scholarship noted aspects of the practice (Chambers 1923, III: 124–5, 130–2, and n). However, these observations remained essentially dots un-joined; when they were (e.g. Smith 1964, 223–30, 301–2) it did not reach the scholarly mainstream. It is in part as a consequence that the pioneering work to which this study is indebted – the foundational scholarship on candle-lighting (Graves 1999, 2009), and the most comprehensive account of the marking of act-divisions (Taylor 1993) – both elide the interval, while nevertheless providing a working scaffold for the present enquiry.

The principal evidence, of course, is the plays themselves. Act-division yields a good deal of information, though its deeper implications for play-making need digging out. The structure of printed drama tells a compelling story, though modern editorial practices often obscure provenance. Amphitheatre plays were usually printed undivided, reflecting original, unin-terrupted staging; similarly, there is a remarkable correlation between plays known to have been performed indoors and the printing of act-divisions, at least before the adult companies began operating regularly in London indoor theatres, first at Blackfriars, and then subsequently at the Cockpit/Phoenix, Salisbury Court, and Cockpit-in-Court. Children's plays provide a good test case. Of 69 printed over the twenty-year period 1588–1609, only five are undivided. Thus, with very few exceptions (none of which could have been staged without intervals indoors), these texts register theatre practice, while the outliers present tricky questions for modern editors, as I discuss at the end of this Element. It was surely clear to playreaders what these structural differences meant in terms of theatre provenance, even if some amphitheatre plays (such as the *Tamburlaine* diptych) reflect faux-classical tradition, deriving from the printing-house, not the playhouse.

This makes a subsequent development all the more significant. In his seminal essay 'The Structure of Performance' Gary Taylor examines how this pattern of difference gave way to a uniform practice: 'Every one of the 245 extant plays written for [the London] companies between 1616 and 1642 (inclusive) is divided into five acts' (Taylor 1993, 4). This remarkable finding leads to a tantalising conclusion, that this is 'positive evidence for regular act-intervals in the later Jacobean and Caroline theatre' (Taylor 1993, 8): that is, *outdoors* as well as indoors. The only other interpretation is that all the agents involved in play publication collectively elected to present plays in a 'classical' format, regardless of provenance and practice.

The import of Taylor's scholarship is threefold. First, there is nothing to indicate that conditions in the amphitheatres altered, so there is no reason to suppose that intervals became *necessary* there. Second, therefore, if they were adopted it was for other reasons, perhaps aesthetic and/or economic, since this would ease the movement of plays between theatre types. It would certainly have been logical for companies that operated in both domains regularly, as did the King's Men from the beginning of the second decade of the 17th century, to implement a uniform structure; but that does not explain why this may have been the case across the board, if it was. It follows, third, then, that if the interval came to transcend its origins it did so for other reasons, which will emerge in the course of this study.

1.3 What the Interval May Tell Us

The argument this Element makes does not depend on Taylor's hypothesis being correct, but it makes it more likely that it is. Although act-breaks provided a solution to a practical problem, they not only gave an added dimension to performance, most notably with respect to the music for which the children's companies were especially famed (see e.g. Munro 2009, 545–51), but provided playwrights with greater flexibility than the amphitheatres afforded. To stand the question on its head, we might consider why outdoor companies would choose *not* to innovate in this way, given its advantages.

To this end the structure of this Element is broadly chronological. The first two parts explore questions arising from the enquiry and the ways playmakers exploited the interval respectively. First, I focus on some of the practical issues relating to indoor theatre architecture and lighting, before sketching the properties of the interval. The section following is concerned with how playmakers wrote specifically *for* indoor conditions. Here I identify invisible and visible traces of the act-time in the surviving corpus.

The historical drift of the early modern theatre is amphitheatre > hall. It is true that the earliest outdoor venues flourished, in several cases (Theatre, Curtain, Rose) for many years, and more were built in the new century: the Fortune (1600), Red Bull (1605), second Globe (1613–1614), and Hope (1614). But a parallel tradition long predated the amphitheatre. It is specifically through shared performance conditions that the later, professional development of the hall theatre may be traced back to entertainments for the elite, for example *Fulgrens and Lucrece* (c.1497), acted for Cardinal Morton; to the chorister-performers of the later 16th century; and, after a hiatus (1590–1599), to the children's companies that emerged in the opening decade of the seventeenth. It might seem that the success of Paul's Boys, and the two royal troupes, the Children of the King's/Queen's Revels, persuaded the adult companies where the future lay. But even before the rise of a resurgent children's theatre the Chamberlain's Men in 1596 invested in an indoor space; they would not succeed for another decade, but it would seem that the Burbages already had a long-term plan that much later other companies would emulate.

The amphitheatre > hall trajectory (and less commonly, vice versa) required textual intervention: in other words, intervals were introduced (or removed). The next section explores marked-up texts and revised plays where adaptation has left traces. The best example of an outdoor-indoor operation is the King's Men, and the final part offers a contribution to the long-standing debate over the impact of the Blackfriars on repertory management, as well as those of several lesser-known troupes. A summation in the Coda brings us back to the theatrical and editorial present, and how we might incorporate the interval in our current, as well as historical, framing of early modern theatre.

2 Candles and Questions

While R.G. Graves has argued recently that artificial lighting played no more than an ancillary role indoors, SWP-related scholarship has stressed the aesthetic aspects of playing by candlelight (White 2014; Dustagheer 2017, 123–38; Tosh 2018, 91–118; Munro 2020, 78–81). According to Graves,

> Records of the times of performances at the professional troupes' hall playhouses consistently refer to the afternoon; the number of candles lit was apparently not large; and the evidence we have indicates the auditoriums were well provided with windows, admitting substantial sunshine.
> (Graves 2009, 529)

In fact, not enough evidence has survived to justify this generalization. As adapted spaces from extant buildings (as is, incidentally, the SWP), London's indoor venues no more conformed to a specific design than did their outdoor counterparts, about which (thanks to their archaeological footprint) we know rather more. Once we include other roofed performance spaces, such as the court, the picture becomes more complicated still.

Pace the SWP's findings – which (unlike Graves's) cannot offer a comparative natural light/candlelight comparison, since the space lacks windows and hence shuts out daylight entirely – it would make sense economically for companies to limit the use of candles, if they were able to do so, which would tally with Graves's argument. While these theatres had much in common in terms of design with Tudor halls (Graves 2009, 539), location and orientation must have affected lighting needs. Graves's calculations work rather better with outdoor playhouses, in the liberties, than with the indoor theatres inside the city walls. The amphitheatres were large structures, and as can be seen in contemporary engravings such as Wenceslas Hollar's *Long View of London from Bankside* (1647), the admission of sunlight was constrained only by their own height and design. With indoor theatres, since they were located in dense areas of the city, proximity to other (possibly taller) buildings may well have affected a sunlight/candlelight ratio; indeed, the situation might change over time, with the erection of new buildings nearby. Thus, if the stage at the Blackfriars was installed on the upper floor (Foakes 1985, 68–9), lighting considerations may have been a factor, and certainly illumination levels would have been affected. Conversely, the rather small windows depicted in the Worcester College, Oxford drawings suggest that (even if the design was never implemented) candle-lighting was expected to play a significant role. The absence of windows in the lower gallery may indicate that 'none was needed' (Graves 1999, 143) – that there was sufficient natural light from the windows above – *or* that the design reflected a desire to reduce or indeed eliminate sunlight in order to emphasize the kind of effect hailed at the SWP. That would appear to be the case with theatrical performances at Cambridge University: college accounts dating from the 15th to the 18th centuries repeatedly detail the expenditure on candles, lamps, and candlesticks, as well as haircloths and nets to cover the windows, shutting out light (Nelson 1994, 33–113). There, plays were mostly staged at night, but in daytime performances the windows were covered; citing REED records, Alan H. Nelson states that 'in 1594–5 the plays were staged, "the day being turned into nyght"; in 1622–3 the hall was "darkened"' (Nelson 1994, 111). The evidence is diverse, and may well reflect different practices. After all, given that existing structures repurposed extant buildings, it is reasonable to suppose that while the *interior* was altered, the structure, including the windows, was not – unless temporarily to darken the auditorium. Dekker's description in *The Seuen deadly Sinnes of London* – 'all the City lookt like a private Playhouse, when the windows are clapt downe, as if some Nocturnal, or dismall *Tragedy* were presently to be acted' (Dekker 1606, D2) – has been taken to indicate that companies used shutters, perhaps even to provide a primitive form of variable lighting appropriate to the genre of the play being performed (Cohen 2009, 216; Graves 2009, 536; White 2014, 117), but whether the players had the resources to open or close or indeed access them at all while the theatre was packed with playgoers is moot (Smith 1964, 302). More likely, as suggested by the REED evidence, if the windows were shuttered this was done at the beginning and remained so for the duration of the performance. If so (and this aligns with recent SWP-related scholarship), the aesthetic effects produced were presumably considered financially worth the candle.

A key factor, certainly, was time of day and year. The Blackfriars, it seems, was only used in winter, while the Salisbury Court staged plays all year round (Graves 2009, 535). If the Blackfriars staged plays in the evening, this entailed higher expenditure on candles (Stern 2014, 108), which winter playing compounded, when it was dusk by four in the afternoon (Graves 1999, 69); if, alternatively, the King's Men performed in the afternoon (Cohen 2009, 216), as was their Globe practice of course, this would have made economic sense, as Tiffany Stern concedes (Stern 2014, 108), though two other factors are relevant: (i) with windows shuttered the candles would have greater effect; and (ii) even if experiments find candlelight to be relatively ineffectual by modern standards (Graves 1999, 125–200), it is worth remembering that early modern spectators were used to lower levels of illumination than people today accustomed to electric light (Cohen 2009, 217n). The notoriously unreliable English weather must have influenced decisions, and it may well be that adjustment in terms of quantity of candles required was made on a daily basis. At the Salisbury Court, at least in the summer, perhaps candles were not necessary at all (Graves 1999, 130), assuming that the windows admitted sufficient light. Conversely, if the King's Men performed in the evening to ape court practice (Stern 2014, 108–14) then for much of its operation the Blackfriars must have been almost entirely dependent on artificial light, the playhouse perhaps 'clapt downe', as per Dekker, to accentuate the effect of playing by candles.

Whether candlelight augmented or supplanted natural light, the quality of the latter declined even where performances began in the afternoon, so with uncovered windows this would be pronounced, particularly over the winter. If there was a lighting/genre correlation, the type of play that was the best fit was tragedy, since the narrative movement towards the denouement would be accompanied by a reduction in *natural* illumination. Perhaps playwrights sometimes composed to the interval, aware that lighting changes might be made then (Gary Taylor, personnel communication), though it is possible that changes to candle illumination were sometimes made mid-scene (as at the SWP; see Tosh 2018, 91–118), and even by the actors themselves – whether in-character or not – for which there is evidence from the

Restoration (Graves 1999, 183). Another, more likely possibility is that portable lights were used, brought on and off by characters (White 1998, 50); indeed, indoor conditions may have influenced composition in this way, dramatists deliberately scripting action accordingly. In *The Dutch Courtesan*, for example, acts 1, 2, and 4 open with characters bringing on lights. But probably the vast majority of lighting modification was done between the acts (White 1998, 149).

As for the candles themselves, one starting point is to assume that higher quality candles (the much more expensive wax) would burn better (more evenly, with fewer structural problems) than tallow, and larger candles would (logically) burn for a longer period of time than smaller ones; but it does not follow that wax or larger candles required less attention than tallow or smaller candles. The principal difference between tallow and wax was the unpleasant smell of the former, so even if higher quality candles burned for longer, they needed regular intervention just the same. Evidence from a 1639 document indicates that both tallow and wax candles were used at Salisbury Court (Bentley 1941–68, VI: 106; qtd. in Graves 2009, 535), though it may be that tallow candles were used to illuminate the tiring-house, rather than the stage. Undoubtedly court spaces, since they were much larger than the hall theatres, required more candles, and could call on more lighting resources than could private theatres – 'nearly ten times as many candles as were available at Salisbury Court' (Graves 2009, 541) – but more candles meant more mending, as well as more illumination.

All things being equal (which they were not), the one constant in any venue that used candles – whether few, in conjunction with sunlight, or many, in its absence – was the need to attend to them, as necessary. 'Classical' dramatic structure provided the obvious solution, as playmakers seem to have recognized; indeed, in a sense amphitheatre practice was a departure from this putative 'norm', and the uniform marking of act-divisions in Jonson's *Workes* (1616, 1641–42), most of the Shakespeare First Folio (1623), and the Beaumont and Fletcher compendium (1647) might thus be considered a form of 'restoration'. Still, important questions remain, some of which are beyond the scope of this study but for which the following offers a starting point.

2.1 The Act-Time: Length/Number

Taking the second of these first: evidence from manuscript and printed texts leaves no room for doubt that the five-act, four-interval structure was employed indoors, with perhaps some support for slight variation at royal palaces or the Inns of Court. If Marston's *Histrio-Mastix* (1598–1599) was in fact written for the Inns of Court, as its enormous casting requirements and otherwise old-fashioned morality format suggests (Finkelpearl 1966), then its division into *six* acts (Q1610) may just register a slightly different arrangement. Performances in the royal palaces, and to a lesser extent at the universities, pose related questions, given the resources at their disposal; but the technology was a great leveller: '[o]n special occasions, the Stuart court used wax in the candles closest to the sovereign . . . ; but typically, king and commoner alike suffered the disagreeable effects of tallow. Only in the reign of Charles I were wax candles widely deployed for the illumination of plays' (Graves 1999, 14–15). But regular candle maintenance was required regardless. Recently Richard Dutton has argued that court patronage best explains why some Shakespeare plays are notably longer than most others in the wider corpus of surviving drama. Challenging the long-standing consensus that plays were cut down for performance, he contends that Q1600 *Henry V*, for example, was added to, producing the First Folio version (or something approximating to it): like other Shakespearean texts, it was revised – that is, made *longer* – for court performance (Dutton 2016). Whatever the merits of this explanation for the varying lengths of a significant number of Shakespeare plays, Dutton does not consider the need for intervals, but as with *Histrio-Mastix* it is possible that conditions at court were indeed more flexible; certainly, the court was not restricted, timewise (Chambers 1: 214–15; qtd. in Dutton 2016, 82). Perhaps, then, F *Henry V*, with its problematic divisions modern editors adjust, like *Histrio-Mastix*, featured *six* act-breaks at court, which the First Folio imperfectly records. But these speculations aside, the evidence for the London venues at least points firmly in the direction of four intervals.

The key finding of this Element is that lighting technology did not overdetermine the issue. Candles required intervals but not vice versa.

Although 'wicks burned unevenly ... [and] had to be snuffed ... [which] was regularly required' (Graves 1999, 14), whether they were snuffed at *every* act-break, or provision was made just in case, is not clear. The technology was unstable, and other factors, as noted, probably affected the number of candles required: the salient point is that act-breaks avoided awkward intrusions into the play-world.

Unsurprisingly, surviving texts tend not to record the actions of tiremen, whose role it was to light and then monitor the candles. One exception is Marston's *What You Will* (Q1607), which begins:

INDVCTION.

> *Before the Musicke sounds for the Acte: Enter* Atticus,
> Doricus,*& * Phylomuse, *they sit a good while on the*
> *Stage before the Can-dles are lighted, talking together,*
> *& on suddeine* Doricus *speakes.*

– followed by '*Enter* Tier-man *with lights*.', whereupon the opening line is spoken, with some knockabout stuff: 'O Fie some lights, sirs fie, let there be no deeds of darkness done among vs. – I so, so, pree thee Tyer-man set *Sineor Snuff* a fier' (A2r). The Induction gives way to the Prologue, and then the play proper begins. As we shall see, Marston is notable for exploiting the theatrical frame in which plays operate, here drawing attention to the lighting (a signal for everyone that the performance is about to begin), but this does not happen more generally at act-breaks, either in *What You Will* or other texts. Here the tireman (or 'Tier-man' or Tyer-man) – who is either a functionary or an actor playing one – is used as a foil; not given an exit, his is a ghost part, central to the indoor operation but rarely recorded. (Conversely, the 'Tyer-man' who opens *Jack Drum's Entertainment* [Q1601, A2r] speaks but does not light candles: clearly, he is an actor, rather than a functionary.) Not perhaps insignificantly, the concern is less with lighting at these points than with how the interval both concealed and exploited its practical function. Occasionally (e.g. the beginning of act 1 of *What You will*; the opening of the second act of *The Malcontent*; and at the beginning of acts 1, 2, and 4 in *The Dutch Courtesan*) *characters* enter with lights; but whether these instances are entirely separate from the stage lighting, remaining within the play-world, or doing double duty, is impossible to ascertain.

In addition to the marking of act-breaks – in manuscript as well as printed texts – further support for the number of intervals derives from information about their length, which nevertheless presents a rather more complicated picture. If the Horace-derived model accommodated any technological problems arising, it does not necessarily follow that each of the four act-breaks was of equal duration, and the (admittedly slight) evidence is suggestive of variation rather than uniformity. But this is not surprising. As scholars note, the commonplace 'measure' of playing time – 'two or three hours' traffic' – was vague and approximate (see Hirrel 2010): not only because plays were of varying length but because for early moderns time-telling was necessarily imprecise. Scholars have not fully appreciated that, indoors, act length (and therefore play length) were determined by candle technology. Thus, plays were composed accordingly (or, in the case of amphitheatre > hall conversion, adjusted); dialogue and stage business must have been carefully reckoned. But while candles ruled in the first instance, the point was to trim the candles, not the interval.

Two forms of evidence indicate that the indoor system was sufficiently adaptable to tolerate variation. The first consists of traces of company or tiring-house activity in preparing the play for the stage. Composed for the King's Men, *Believe As You List* (MS1631) survives in holograph and is particularly valuable because it shows the work of the company book-keeper, Edward Knight. At just over 2,400 lines it is almost evenly divided, at 500, 505, 495, 479, and 424 lines respectively. But Knight marks two of the act-breaks as 'Act:/Long' (1/2) and 'long Act: 4' (3/4), which implies that the other two were short(er). The same descriptor appears in a marked-up quarto (Q1620) of *The Two Merry Milkmaids* ('Longe' at 1/2), and in an early Thomas Heywood play, *1 Fair Maid of the West* (c.1597–1603?), 'Act long' at 4/5 (Q1631 showing it had been revived for staging indoors, along with a newly composed sequel). Whatever their local purpose(s), they suggest a pattern; how general can only be speculated.

A further group offers another kind of variation. Beaumont's *The Knight of the Burning Pestle* (1607) and Jonson's *The Staple of News* (1626) and *The Magnetic Lady* (1632) all populate each of the four intervals with scripted business integral to the design, as will be discussed in the next section. However, these sequences are of unequal length, running (in modern editions: Zitner 1984; Parr 1988; Happé 2000) to 12/18/17/62 lines, 79/69/56/87, and 70/85/38/36 respectively (Hutchings 2013, 271; White 2018, 319n). Clearly, there is no correlation here between technological requirements and act-time length: once the interval was decoupled from its *practical* function it could be repurposed as a facilitator of compositional and performative innovation. Where Beamont and Jonson make use of each of the act-breaks, another example illustrates a stark asymmetry in how the interval might be used. If modern editors are correct in reordering text in Middleton's *Your Five Gallants* (Q1608), at 2/3 two 'interims' featured, of 27 and 95 lines respectively – plus act-time music, so that Tailby can exit and re-enter at the beginning of act 3 (which the Oxford Middleton editors do not consider), a playmaking convention I discuss later. Even without this music these units would seem to constitute the longest known interval, which contrasts starkly with the other three in Middleton's play, otherwise unmarked and presumably in relative terms generic. As with the Beamont, Jonson, and indeed other examples, it may well be that here 'the boundary between act-interval and act is entirely blurred' (Taylor and Lavagnino 2007b, 576). Indeed, at 3/4 *The Knight of the Burning Pestle* the text gives 'Boy daunceth' (Q1613, G4v), and the dancing boy is incorporated into the action.

2.2 Candles +

Thus, practical experiments with candles in modern environments, such as the SWP, miss the point somewhat, and the assumption that 'the prime function of the interval was to manage the lighting' (White 2014, 126n) takes us only so far. The picture revealed by the surviving corpus is rather more intriguing.

Early modern theatre architecture determined that breaks in the action would necessarily constitute a component of the theatre experience – functioning, as we shall see, as a *unit* of the play-as-event, whether (as a number of examples attest) diegetic, within the play-world, or (more commonly, though ambiguously) non-diegetic, on the plane of performance. But playmakers were faced with what to do with this visual-temporal sequence that took place in full view of the audience. Here music played a key role.

First as hosts of children's drama, and subsequently featuring adult troupes, these venues were small, musical theatres that enveloped the play in sound; to grasp the aural aspect of the interval we need to situate act-breaks in relation to the soundscape of these places, as well as in terms of its function in the performance. Here the play was both framed and divided by musical accompaniment, this music – usually, it seems, if not always, accompanied by a dancing boy – providing aural-visual 'cover' for the tireman to check the candles (or darken or lighten the stage, as may be). But it did more than this. Unfortunately, the music itself has not survived, a further example of the 'documents of performance' Tiffany Stern identifies as components of the staging, though not always printing, of early modern drama (Stern 2009, 120–73). But we can be fairly certain that music usually featured at each act-break, as is indicated in the Whitefriars play *The Dumb Knight* (Q1607), for example; the plot for *The Dead Man's Fortune*, and extant children's plays, supports this (Taylor 1993, 8–9). That said, where music is signalled at only one interval (e.g. the Children of the King's Revels' *Cupid's Whirligig*, Q1607), we must allow that, within a putative norm, there were exceptions. None of the Beaumont or Jonson plays mentioned earlier signal music, for example, but they are exceptional in featuring scripted dialogue. Generally speaking, at a practical level the sounding of music (and then its cessation) marked the end of one act and the beginning of the next respectively – for those on either side of the tiring-house wall.

The most interesting question, however, upon which we can only speculate, is how this feature related to the play itself: that is, to its conception, performance, and reception. Was the music (and dancing) generic, and so reusable, between plays (and perhaps within or even across repertories); and, if so, was the same music (and dance) used at each of the four intervals? Or, conversely, was the arrangement designed or moulded to fit the genre of the play (as some scholars have speculated with regard to lighting), and perhaps within the play varied according to the narrative trajectory – reflecting and constituting *mood*? Lynda Phyllis Austern connects the children's companies' dual expertise, satire and music, detecting the 'emergence of musical irony' at the beginning of the 17th century (Austern 1985–86, 474), which might well be applied to the interval. Alternatively, might there be no connection with the play-world narrative at all? In other words, as in contemporary French, Spanish, and Italian theatre, there was no relation to the play itself, it functioned as a diversion (as would come to be the case in the modern theatre: curtain down and lights up in the auditorium). Was the interval, then, 'inside' or 'outside' – or did it deconstruct (or resist) this binarism? Certainly, for the audience music was part of the theatre event, and may well have influenced their understanding of the fiction, incidentally or by design.

That indoors (as outdoors) plays featured music as part of the action – whether offstage, performed by musicians, or onstage, by characters in the fiction – might offer a clue: ordinarily, it may be that the interval-music was formally as well as functionally different. In a re-evaluation of where music was actually produced, Simon Smith draws attention to 'music's contribution not just as sound but as sight' (Smith 2017, 31). Given that the displaying of musical performance is theatrically arresting, it makes sense that the musicians were not simply hidden from view, at least not all of the time. Although keen to move away from the established view that music usually emanated from a 'music room' on the upper stage, Smith acknowledges Richard Hosley's suggestion that musicians were concealed behind curtains which opened 'between the acts and before and after the play' (Hosley 1966, 115; qtd. in Smith 2017, 36). In distinctively musical plays – such as Marston's *Sophonisba* (Q1606) – visual distinction may have been made between offstage music during the play itself and the act-time accompaniment. This is purely speculative, of course, but Hosley's hypothesis that interval-music was always staged above, framed by an open and closed curtain (Hosley 1966, 116–17), is attractive. If the musicians were revealed, performed, and then were concealed by a curtain, all this in sync with the dancing boy and tireman below, such coordination would have given the act-time a unifying definition – visually, aurally, temporally.

Measured against the surviving corpus, *Sophonisba* is unrepresentative, but it illustrates what was considered possible, and it may be that, although the music itself has not survived, Marston's play preserves evidence of wider practice; certainly, this is the case regarding the scripting of the act-time (at 1/2 and 2/3). Q sets out how particular instruments are specified for each of four act-breaks:

The Ladies draw the curtaines about *Sophonisba*,
the rest accompany *Massinissa* forth, the
Cornets and *Organs* playing loud
full Musicke for the Act.

Actus Primi.

FINIS.

Actus Secundi.

Scena Prima.

Whil'st the Musicke for the first *Act* soundes *Hanno, Car-*
thalo, By:heas, Gelosso enter: They place themselues to
Counsell, *Giseo* th'impoisner waiting on them, *Han-*
no, Carthalo, and *Bytheas*, setting their hands
to a writing, which being offer'd to
Gelosso, he denies his hand, and
as much offended impati-
ently starts vp and
speakes.

(B3v)

Giue me some health, now your bloud sinkes: thus deedes
Illnourisht rot, without Ioue naught succeedes. Exeunt.
Actus Secundi. Finis.

Organ mixt with Recorders for this Act.

A*ctus Tertii, Scena Prima.*

Syphax his dagger twon about her haire drags in *So-*
Phonisba in hir nightgowne petticoate and *Zanthia* &
Vaugue following.

(D2 r-v)

3/4

With a full florish of Cornettes they depart.

Actus Tertii

FINIS.

Organs Violls and Voices
play for this Act.

Actus Quarti Scena Prima.

Enter Sophonisba and Zanthia as out of a caues mouth

(E2v)

4/5

Syphax hasteneth within the Canopy as to Sophonisbas bed

Actus Quarti.

FINIS.

A Base Lute and a Treble Violl
play for the Act:

Actus Quinti Scena Prima.

Syphax drawes the curtaines and discouers Erichtho lying with him.
(F2r)

That *Sophonisba* features music at numerous other junctures, at the beginning of as well as within scenes – the 'Prologus' opens with, and the play is regularly punctuated by, the cornet – invites speculation about how the act-time music excerpted here related to the play-narrative 'score'. How did the play's 'subtle orchestration of music' (Corbin and Sedge 1986, 5) operate? Each interval – '*Cornets and organs*' (1/2), '*Organ mixt with Recorders*' (2/3), '*Organs Violls and Voices*' (3/4), and '*A Base Lute and a Treble Violl*' (4/5) – is given a musical signature (the absence of the music itself notwithstanding).

Even without diegetic and non-diegetic music elsewhere in the play, it might reasonably be supposed that each of these four arrangements (three featuring the organ, a physically substantial instrument) were grouped together, most likely in the gallery stage 'music room', thus differentiating – visually as well as aurally – the act-time from the on-/offstage aural accompaniment in the play itself, and perhaps providing the 'musical irony' Austern identifies in the children's drama. At 3/4, for example, the stage is cleared to 'a full flourish of trumpets', followed by the act-time '*Organs Violls and Voices*'. Whether or not the act-time instrumentation did occupy an in-between place, the music room being neither wholly onstage nor offstage, it straddled diegetic/non-diegetic spheres.

2.3 Imagining the Act-Time

If it were possible to sum up the interval, 'in-betweenness' would be a good starting point. Not only in the sense of structural punctuation at four points in the play-narrative, but along all the axes through which this theatre operated. To consider whether the act-time is 'inside' or 'outside' the play is in a sense to ask the wrong question, for we cannot abstract 'the play' from the theatre event. The Latinate in-betweenness of 'interval' or 'intermission' implies the *suspension* of performance, but such a notion would have been alien to those who frequented the Whitefriars or Salisbury Court. The *OED*'s first theatre-specific reference to this usage – from Pepys's *Diary*, 'I . . . talked to them all intervalls of the play' – is not until 1667 (*OED*, 'interval, *n*', 1. a); the word does feature in Cotgrave's English and French *Dictionary* (1611), but as a measure of time between events, not in relation to theatre. Crucially, how language accommodated the emergence of a new facet of indoor performance – which we may tentatively date to sometime in the 16th century, with the rise of children's playing and their proficiency in music – is revealing; the 'intervall' of Pepys's time, unsurprisingly, registers recent political events, even if it may also suggest a post-Interregnum evolution in theatre practice. Earlier, the sense is of fluidity in theatrical performance, rather than hiatus, 'act' doing double duty, both as classical unit, where the *OED* cites Terence in print in c.1520 (*OED*, 'act, n', II.9.a.), *and*, giving several examples from 1606 onwards, the music that punctuated the five-act dramatic structure indoors (*OED*, II.9.b.); Cotgrave, tellingly, gives for 'act', 'Pause in a Comedie or Tragedie' (qtd. in Taylor 1993, 10): the lexical porosity of 'act'/'act-time' captures nicely how in performance the play-world bleeds into (and out of) the 'pause'. This is theatre as Venn Diagram, formally, spatially, temporally, textually.

This terminological overlap registers a fluidity that was a function of the indoor theatre, its architecture and its practices: act > (-time) > act. Unlike the amphitheatre, open to the skies with a raised stage separated from the audience, in the smaller, intimate indoor playhouse comparatively firm distinctions outdoors – acting-arena, audience-space – were blurred, and this difference was underscored by the act-time. The practice of stage-sitting was pivotal. From a modern perspective, a notional stage (actor)/auditorium (audience) binary, such as we find outdoors, was subjected to forces that affected the status of both constituencies. The stage was no longer exclusively the preserve of actors, as is understood to have been the case in the amphitheatres (exceptions proving the rule: Thomson 2010); and the audience was not confined to a non-performance space. Although stage-sitting involved relatively few spectators, it was symbolically significant out of proportion to its numbers. Not only was the custom a visual reminder of a shift in authority, in which (we may conjecture) the stage became a site of at least implicit contest for space between actor and spectator (and between spectators themselves), but those who paid extra for a stool entered from the tiring-house – at a stroke disrupting the relationship between role and space. This authorized access – first *into* the tiring-house, before the play begins (perhaps using the same door as the actors, as distinct from the theatre entrance by which the audience came in), and then ostentatiously *entering the stage* – conferred a privilege stage-sitters would fully exploit during the act-time. For this we have evidence in both paratextual material and metatheatrical scripting of business, as we shall see. Like Pepys later, many of these stage-sitters 'talked to [other spectators] all intervalls of the play', but they did so in an environment where, the stage cleared of actors (if not a dancing boy), it was now an ambiguous, fluid space.

An aural and visual, spatial and temporal porosity is also evident in the design of plays. While the majority of surviving texts ostensibly appear to leave the act-time to functionaries in the tiring-house, in a number of cases the play continues to flow, from one act to the next, through the interval and out the other side. John Marston seems to have begun his career working for Henslowe's amphitheatre operation, before writing exclusively for indoor performance; ironically, while on the basis of surviving evidence he is the most innovative of the hall playwrights, his scripting of the interval, in plays such as *Sophonisba*, and others discussed shortly, suggests a hybrid ampthitheatre-hall approach. Here, Marston and others, rather than ceding *play*-time to the act-time, continue the action, even though the act has nominally concluded; or, conversely, during the interval, action begins that segues into the next act; or, alternatively, the act-time serves as a self-contained unit – a mini-scene, as it were – as in Middleton and Rowley's *The Changeling* at 2/3. What *does* complicate this narrative continuity is a shift in form, from scripted dialogue in the body of the play to dumb show in the act-time, as we shall see.

The big (unanswerable) question is how such moments signified. Playgoers must have become accustomed to the convention of music, dancing, and candle-mending that provided the cue for spectators to 'stand down' – or stand *up*, in the case of stage-sitters –but in being temporarily released from their role as audience they might occasionally find themselves wrong-footed. How to read *intrusions* into the act-time – when the *play* 'trespasses'? First, if playmakers intended that act-time business was integral to the play they could not guarantee that spectators distracted by audience behaviour (or their own) would notice. Second, it may be that this was partly the point: that the act-time offered the opportunity to explore different kinds of theatrical effect. There is something of the uncanny in the scripting of 2/3 in *The Changeling*, a piece of stage business that could have been carried out at the end or beginning of the respective acts, but which was (according to Q1653) deliberately staged during the interval (Hutchings 2011, 101). After all, De Flores's hiding of the murder weapon he will retrieve is, curiously, the placing of a stage property we associate with tiring-house activity, even though it fits the villainy of his character. Such uses of the act-time – repeatedly by Marston – suggest a conscious rationale that is partly aesthetic in design, partly plot driven: the interval as threshold between play-world and tiring-house. This points to a deployment – and perhaps recognition – of what has come to be understood as *affect* in early modern theatre: that scripting the act-time in this way was considered particularly powerful, since it operated in a different register. Thus, at four points in the play-narrative, a space opens up, albeit temporarily, where (from our 'default-amphitheatre' perspective at least) the terms of engagement shift. To read these plays with intervals in mind, then, is to imagine the in-betweenness of the act-time, not only in plays designed for indoor performance but also those adapted from amphitheatre texts, which in turn raises questions about repertory management, treated in Sections 3, 4, and 5 respectively.

3 Scripting the 'Act-Time'

Plays where the interval is scripted as part of the narrative fiction offer the most arresting and, ostensibly, the best evidence for this Element; but the wider picture – more subtle, less immediately detectable – is perhaps of greater significance. Initially, lack of visibility suggests that exploitation of the interval was rather niche and exceptional. But in fact, playmakers writing specifically for indoor performance did rather more than calculate where in the course of the play-narrative four breaks in the action might fall. First, I explore how, unadorned, the interval could be used structurally, before moving on to plays where it is incorporated into the play-narrative itself.

3.1 The 'Unscripted' Interval

In every play, amphitheatre or hall, an offstage 'continuity text' shadowed what was presented – and presentable – onstage; these locations were connected to the rest of the play-world, offstage (Fitzpatrick 2011; Womack 2013). Playwrights could choose what to show or (instead) tell – except with sexual activity. Thus, rape in amphitheatre plays such as *Titus Andronicus* and *Women Beware Women* had to take place behind the *scene*, while simultaneously the onstage action resumed. In the indoor theatre the act-time brought the offstage temporarily *into* the play-world narrative. For example, the rape of Beatrice-Joanna in *The Changeling* takes place offstage, *during* 3/4. At the end of act 3 the audience is prepared for what will happen, and the beginning of act 4 brings confirmation, the audience invited first, during the interval, to imagine what is taking place beyond the *frons scenae*, and then to reflect on events as the play resumes. Thus is the rape evoked; in a sense it *is* performed, portrayed obliquely and grotesquely through the interval music and dancing – and, crucially, in the imagination of the audience: freed from its attention to onstage action, it is invited (if not compelled) to bring the offstage into play. In *'Tis Pity She's a Whore* Giovanni and Anabella exit at the end of the penultimate scene of act 1 to consummate their love, and re-enter at the beginning of the second act, '*as from their Chamber*' (Q1633, C3v) – a whole scene *and* the interval taken up by their consensual incest. The length of *actual* time they spend 'in bed', offstage, surely registered with the audience, and Ford may have been playing with the convention for macabre/comic effect.

In these and other examples the offstage is a *place*. If 'the (implied) presence of the offstage space always functions as ... an unrepresentable invisibility behind the wall' (Turner 2006, 29) – which, in effect posits the play *itself* as a seamless *wall* that demarcates onstage and offstage as distinct entities – we might consider that the act-time breaches this barrier. For in such instances it is the *onstage* play that 'pauses', bringing into the audience's orbit its offstage continuation, as the stage is cleared. In a play such as *The Changeling*, where the onstage action 'is typically set somewhere outside a closed and significant room' (Womack 2019, 95), it is in the act-time especially that partial access to these offstage spaces is facilitated, through an imaginative engagement with the continuity narrative.

Modern productions that show sex/sexual violence on stage miss the structural and symbolic function of the act-time, and appreciation of it might usefully inform performance-centred criticism. We should properly speak, then, not of five-act plays but of five-act/four-interval drama (Hutchings 2023, 45–6). Indoors, a play never 'hesitates' as such: we do indeed need to learn to read 'between the acts' (Taylor 1993, 3).

3.2 The 'Law of Re-entry' and 'Enter *[...]* / Exeunt *[...]* Severally'

Even less visible, since only through familiarity with theatre practices are the traces left discernible, two related aspects of stagecraft common to both types of theatre illustrate how the act-time influenced the construction of plays. Put simply, breaks in the action rendered the stage architecture more flexible than was the case in the amphitheatres, increasing entrance/exit permutations and thus affording playwrights additional compositional options.

Drawing on an observation made more than a century ago now, Irwin Smith noted that 'Shakespeare avoided having a character enter the stage at the beginning of an act or scene after having been on-stage at the end of the preceding act or scene' (Smith 1967, 8n, 7). Smith's concern is with apparent anomalies in the Shakespeare canon, so his focus is on the amphitheatre, where

> with act following hard upon act and scene upon scene, the player who departed at the end of an act or scene and then reentered at the beginning of the next, would be reentering immediately. ... [which] could only seem futile and bewildering. Presumably the player departed in the first instance in order to accomplish some dramatic purpose, perhaps to make an imaginary behind-the-scenes journey. ... if the player returned immediately, his reentry necessarily denied that any time had elapsed, ... [so] his going and his returning were made to seem meaningless and confusing. (Smith 1967, 7)

Modified slightly, a character *could* re-enter, but only if 'enter[ing] in different company than he departed in' (Taylor 1979, 95) – since this would imply that time had passed, the character having encountered (offstage) another group of people. But the essential principle stands. The 'Law of Re-entry' (LRE) preserved the integrity of the relationship between onstage and offstage, which was constituted by character movement, into and out of the performed action. In the amphitheatre playwrights sometimes got around the LRE by giving a character required for the beginning of the next scene an exit just before the end of the present scene; another character or characters would close the scene, and exit; then, the new scene would begin, with the required character entering. Nevertheless, it remained a structuring principle of playmaking that in large part explains why *every* play consisted of more than one plot, scenes interlaced, the onstage action underpinned by the parallel continuity text offstage.

In the absence of authorial papers with an amphitheatre provenance surviving in any number it is impossible to ascertain whether dramatists regarded this convention as a *problem* as such; but the data presented at the end of this study makes clear that playmakers took advantage of indoor conditions to circumvent the LRE. Irwin Smith had previously alluded to the custom in his Blackfriars study, where he cites several interval-related instances (Smith 1964, 225–8). He showed that, with a new act *not* 'following hard upon act', characters could reappear if required. Thus, the interval could be used like (but more economically than) an intervening scene. *The Tempest* (1611), to be discussed later, is the best-known example, but there are many. Smith was right to assert that this 'LRE-interval' pattern 'constitutes a hitherto unexplored indication that act intermissions were customary in the private playhouses but not in the public' (Smith 1964, 226); but its significance was not appreciated following his 1964 study, or after the essay published three years later: only when we distinguish between indoor and outdoor practices does the importance of the LRE and its implications become apparent.

Entering after an interval was not a re-entry at all. Whatever its length, it seems that the act-time was of sufficient duration for the LRE to be disabled – *actual* as well as play-time having passed – so that the same plotline, through one or more characters, could continue between the end of one act and the beginning of the next. Undoubtedly this influenced play composition, narrative momentum being maintained, rather than interrupted by a parallel plotline; here, the act-time provided continuity, rather than disruption. Its evident appeal is borne out by the data, which is so substantial that it was evidently a shared indoor practice across companies. For example, of the King's Revels Children's repertory of seven plays written for the Whitefriars, three (*Cupid's Whirligig*, 4/5; *The Family of Love*, 2/3; *Humour Out of Breath*, 1/2) use the act-time in this way: a small sample, admittedly, but the ratio increased with the King's Men later (see Appendix). That it features in a Caroline amateur play, *The Humorous Magistrate* (2/3), associated with the Newdigate family in Warwickshire (Kidnie 2012, ix) is perhaps indicative of a wider appreciation of the utility of the act-break outside London.

Its compositional advantages had corresponding disadvantages when plays moved between venue types. While outdoor plays that invariably observed the LRE could be staged indoors, indoors > outdoors movement

presented difficulties, as we shall see with *The Malcontent*. Any indoor >
outdoor conversion featuring a particular sd only possible indoors faced
similar issues. One form of choreographing on-/offstage movement, '*Enter*
[. . .] */Exeunt* [. . .] *severally*', is not exclusive to the indoor theatre (since it
could also be used mid-scene *anywhere*) but the interval made it distinctive.
'*Severally*', as the phrase '*at several doors*' makes clear, means 'separately'
(Dessen and Thomson 1999, 192–3): simultaneous exeunt/entry through
different doors. It is generally agreed that two flanking doors provided the
entry/exit points for the majority of stage/tiring-house movement;
a central opening, upper-stage, and trapdoor *may* have been available at
most or all playhouses but they were used sparingly, accentuating their
effect (see Gurr and Ichikawa 2000; Ichikawa 2002, 2012; Fitzpatrick 2011).
This reliance on two 'opposing' doors had significant implications.
Typically, at the end of *scenes* (indoors as well as outdoors) only one
door was used to clear the stage: a single remaining character would thereby
exit, and the next scene (via the other door) could begin; or, two or more
characters exited, through the same door; or, characters used both doors,
the exits staggered so that the door used first in the sequence remained
'clear' for the next scene. Apart from entrances/exits using the central
opening, these variations characterize how playmakers choreographed the
scene.

Since the interval made *all* exit/entry points available at the end/
beginning of acts, its value for dramatists is obvious. For example, it
made it possible for two characters to depart through different doors –
implicitly (and legibly for the audience) to different destinations – or,
alternatively, meet on stage, arriving from different (offstage) places,
which an entrance through *separate* doors implied. Sometimes the sd is
explicit. In Shirley's *The Doubtful Heir* (1638), at the end of act 3 Rofania
and Ferdinand '*Exeunt severally*' (Q1652, D4v). Middleton and Rowley use
the interval in this way at the beginning of act 2 in *The Changeling*: '*Enter
Beatrice and Jasperino severally*' (Q1653, C3r). As with the end of act 4 in
Shirley's play, where Rofania and Ferdinand clearly go their separate ways
under a generic '*Exeunt*' (E4v), many more examples are inferable. For
example, when Alibius, Isabella, Lollio, and the Madmen and Fools exit at
the end of act 4 of *The Changeling* (G4v), or, where Ferdinand, Bosola,

Duchess, Cariola, and Servants all enter together (3/4, allowing Bosola to circumvent the LRE) at the beginning of act 4 in *The Duchess of Malfi* (I1r): given the respective contexts, they probably do so through separate doors. Thus, the act-time influenced composition, which in turn shaped the narrative. Such 'silent' use of the interval partly explains its invisibility in scholarship, and without guidance modern readers are oblivious its significance – a challenge that might be taken up by modern editors (see Coda).

How the use of both doors, either side of the act-break, affected the interval itself is a nice question. We may speculate that the tireman, and the boy who danced to the accompanying music, entered and then exited through the central opening – indeed, this may have been a convention, given that they are on a different 'plane' to that of the play-world; if so, it would make sense for the stage-sitters, entering before the play began, to do likewise, though in the few instances where their entrance is mentioned the entry-point is not specified.

3.3 The Dumb Show Interval

Rather more visible is a device that depended above all on spectacle. The dumb show, a sequence of mimed action of varying duration, offered dramatists economy, since ceremonies or processions could be represented dialogue-free. Moreover, since in most instances instruments were too loud to allow simultaneous, overlaid dialogue (Van Kampen 2017, 33–4), but became a staple of the act-time, the interval dumb show in a sense was a logical outcome of the scripting of act-breaks. Its close relations are the English masque and civic pageantry (Mehl 1965, 12–14), but the suggestion that it was perhaps influenced by the Italian *intermedii* (Chambers 1923, I: 185) gains traction once we note its associations with the interval. With the exception of the Inigo Jones-designed pastoral *Florimène* at Whitehall in 1635 with its *intermedii* (Foakes 1985, 77), where successively Winter, Spring, Summer, and Autumn appear at the act-breaks (recalling the *intermedii* in Italy, Spanish *entremeses*, and French *entr'actes*, which functioned as playful and discrete diversions from the play proper), the English interval dumb show is always part of the play-world.

Over time the dumb show would come to feature at any stage in a play, but its earliest appearances point to a later function a small number of plays (notably Marston's) record. Several, staged at indoor venues (Inner Temple, court), deploy it as central to both the structure and the argument. In *Gorboduc* (1562), *Jocasta* (1566), *The Misfortunes of Arthur* (1588), and *Tancred and Gismund* (1591) it has a didactic function, introducing the main theme and, in prefacing each of the five acts, guiding the audience's engagement (see Mehl 1965, 30–59); *Locrine* (c.1585–1586/c.1590–1594), whose provenance is uncertain, is similarly structured. Naturally, these examples of elaborate tableaux had a 'literary' purpose; however, their continuation through theatre history was assured not in the face of changing taste and fashion, but due to the underlying function of the interval. At its most fundamental such interval business corresponded to one dumb show definition as 'where one or more characters advance and retire without having spoken' (Mehl 1965, xii). A particularly intriguing example, discussed at length elsewhere (Hutchings 2011), occurs in *The Changeling*, where, at the beginning of act 3 (and immediately following the entrance of Alonzo and De Flores) the earliest quarto gives '(*In the Act time Deflores hides a naked Rapier*.)' (Q1653, D3v) That is, at 2/3 a minimalist dumb show takes place, prior to the next sequence where De Flores retrieves his sword and murders Alonzo. Rather more elaborate is *The Fatal Dowry* (1617–1619), at 2/3 the text reading: 'Hoboyes. / *Here a passage over the Stage, while the Act is playing / for the Marriage of Charalois with / Beaumelle, etc*' (Q1632, F1r). Whatever this 'passage' (and personnel) entailed, it was legible as a procession and efficient in maintaining momentum; it portrays something that is important to the plot (a marriage), but the play's focus is its *consequences*. Viewed in this way, the scripting of the act-time in *Sophonisba* is a striking example of the interval dumb show. Music heralds a dumb show that provides a visual backdrop for the prologue; some characters remain on stage, as the play begins. This pattern of action straddling the play's act-divisions continues with the dumb show at 1/2, and possibly at 2/3, where a brief dumb show may indicate that the 'line' between the act-time and beginning of act 3 was opaque in performance. 3/4 appears straightforward, but the use of 4/5 to evade the LRE suggests a degree of continuity across the act-break. Marston had a penchant for exploiting the act-time in this way.

Antonio's Revenge (1600) features lengthy dumb shows (too long to quote here) at 1/2, 2/3, and 4/5; in each case the act/interval 'division' is visually porous, the music providing an aural frame.

Elsewhere, the absence of musical cues is not necessarily evidence of absence. Almost certainly the following Marston dumb shows would have been accompanied by music:

The Malcontent, 1/2:

ACTVS SECVUNDUS. SCE. PRIMA.

Enter Mendozo *with a Sconce, to obserue* Fernezes *entrance,*
who whilst the Act is playing: Enter vnbraced 2. Pages
before him with lights, is met by Maquerelle *and*
conuaide in. The Dutches Pages
sent away.

(C3v)

The Fawn, 4/5:

ACTVS QVINTVS.

Whilest the Act is playing, Hercules and Tiberio enters, Tibe-
rio climbs the tree, and is received aboue by Dulcimel, Philoca-
lia and a Priest: Hercules stayes beneath.

(H3r)

What You Will, 2/3:

Act.3. SCAE. I.

Enter Francisco *halfe drest, in his black doublet and round cap, the*
the [sic] *rest riche,* Iacomo *bearing his hatte and feather?* Adrean *his*
doublet and band, Randolfo *his cloake and staffe: they cloath*
Francisco, *whilst* Bydet *creepes in and obserues them. Much of*
of [sic] *this done whilst the Acte is playing.*

(D3r)

Whether or not music *was* used, it is surely unlikely a dancing boy was retained, since his role was superfluous, and would undermine the legibility of the stage business. It would seem, then, that there was a variety of practice. '*Much of this done whilst the Acte is playing*' suggests not only act>(-time)> act porosity but perhaps also a degree of improvisation or flexibility).

Measured against the total number of act-breaks in surviving plays, these examples are outliers. But this might not be the full story. Some printed plays (such as *The Spanish Tragedy*) announce a dumb show but only the cue is given, not the *text*; as Tiffany Stern argues, it would seem that dumb shows were detached – then re-attached in the printing house, if they reached the printer (Stern 2018, 27–8). Like prologues, epilogues, and choruses – 'which were as likely as not from a different date to that of the playtext' – dumb show intervals might be categorised as 'interims', additions to the play proper (Stern 2009, 108, 107–9). *Endimion*, for example, was first published in 1591, but only in a later printing (Q1632) does additional material appear, including a dumb show seemingly at the end of act 2 (Stern 2018, 24–7). In fact, this looks very much like an interval dumb show at 2/3, rather than end-act business. Where the Marston examples place act-time business at the beginning of the new act (like the *Changeling* dumb show interval), others, such as Lyly's play, put it at the end of the previous act: a reminder that the mise-en-page itself posed problems, a point to which I will return at the end of this Element.

That dumb shows seem to have been material additions, separate from the scripted play, and given that the author of a dumb show was not always responsible for the play itself (Mehl 1965, 6; Stern 2018, 27–8), there may well be further implications for our understanding of the provenance of intervals. The question how these, often elaborate, sequences were prepared (Thomson 2016) leads Stern to conclude that group rehearsals were necessary – which in turn would have depended on 'separate papers aside from the play' (Stern 2018, 28–31, 29). Taking all these factors together it is conceivable that sometimes or generally the company was responsible for the design and choreography of the act-time – not the dramatist(s). If so, following Stern it is possible, perhaps likely, that – as with dumb shows that exist only as generic title rather than text – an unknown number of extant printed plays do not record interval business that was originally part of the performance. It is overstating the case to claim that 'dumb shows convey the same information twice', and thus are not essential to a play (Stern 2018, 20) – that is not the case with the interval business cited here – but the authorial/material separateness of the dumb show does make it possible that some act-time activity was devised by the company. Adding to the act-time, beyond the 'standard' music and dancing boy, may have been a temptation that players, as well as playwrights, sometimes could not resist.

3.4 Scripting Stage-Sitting

Another kind of 'addition' was adopted by some playgoers, the interval a catalyst for behaviour associated specifically – though perhaps not exclusively (Thomson 2010) – with the indoor theatre. Looking back, late in the Interregnum, Thomas May recalled:

> I should go to see a Play in *Black-Fryers*: and there . . . I enter'd the *Theater*, and sat upon the Stage . . . I stood up also at the end of every Act, to salute those, whom I never saw before. (May 1657, H3v–H4v; qtd. in Bentley 1941–68, VI: 11)

This account echoes Fitzdottrell in *The Devil is an Ass* (1616) –

> Today, I goe to the *Black fryers Play-House*,
> Sit i' the view, salute all my acquaintance,
> Rise vp between the *Acts*'. (qtd. in Bentley 1941–68, VI: 10)

– but both are benign, compared to Dekker's satire *The Guls Horne-Book* (1609). In 'How a Gallant should behave himself in a Play-house', the stage-sitter is advised how best to disgrace the dramatist:

> in the middle of his play . . . you rise with a skreud and discontented face from your stool to be gone . . . : and, beeing on your feete, sneake not away like a coward, but salute all your gentle acquaintance . . . and draw what troope you can from the stage after you. (Dekker 1609, E4r; qtd. in Thomson 2013, 176)

It seems Dekker was not exaggerating for effect. Two decades later, in his dedication to a play that had failed on the stage, *The New Inn* (1631), Jonson condemns those for whom the appeal of the theatre is:

> To see, and to be seen ... to possess the Stage against the Play: To dislike all, but mark nothing. And by their confidence of rising between the Acts, in Oblique Lines, make *Affadavit* to the whole House, of their not understanding one Scene. (Jonson 1631, Aaaaaal[r]; qtd. in Thomson 2013, 176)

It caused friction among playgoers, too, and in 1639 the king banned the practice at Salisbury Court (Gurr 2004, 36). Print gave playwrights an opportunity to respond, but otherwise when the stage was vacated by the actors, stage-sitters could exploit the privileged position they had, in full view of the audience.

In three surviving plays two playwrights offer one approach to the 'problem', as Jonson, Dekker, and perhaps other playmakers regarded it. Beaumont and Jonson – the former rather more playfully than the latter – took a further step by encompassing the stage-sitters as part of the play: the fiction was extended to the limits (and beyond) of the physical stage space, not only as an act of reclamation but as a provocative appropriation of audience response. The best-known of these, *The Knight of the Burning Pestle* (1607), has been much discussed; *The Staple of News* (1626) and *The Magnetic Lady* (1632) less so. The importing of paratextual-authorial material invites speculation about quite how these plays were staged, given their metatheatrical ambition and the established authority of the playgoing gallants.

When the King's Men's put on *The Malcontent* at the Globe in 1604 they added an Induction that poked fun at the stage-sitting at the Blackfriars. Three years later *The Knight of the Burning Pestle* returned the compliment: a belated riposte, perhaps. In both cases scholars note that the spine of the joke is social class, a tension that would be exploited frequently in city comedy but which here signalled each theatre's social identity, too. In Beaumont's play the Induction scenario extends not only to the intervals but runs through the entire performance. Like the Globe's revised

Malcontent, the text presents *The Knight of the Burning Pestle* as framed, metatheatrically, as a component of the broader theatre event that begins even before the play starts (and ends after it finishes); indeed, a further frame is implied, the practice at the Blackfriars of providing a musical preamble, which the Duke of Stettin-Pomerania mentions in 1602 as lasting for an hour (Chambers 1923, II: 46–7).

The play begins with three out-of-place citizen characters entering symbolically from the theatre audience to sit on the stage – *not*, as was customary, from within the tiring-house; pointedly, their role as stage-sitters is not restricted to the four intervals, their mode of entry suggestive of a social faux pas that will manifest itself in metatheatrical transgression. While this disruption is social as much as dramatic and dramatic because it is socially dissonant, in structural terms Beaumont clearly aimed at fluency as well as interruption. Strikingly, the interlopers are not contained or restricted, despite the Prologue's censure, for not only do they deliver the Epilogue but they interrupt the action at points throughout the five acts. Dramatic structure is key here. Each act consists of a single, unbroken sequence – a design obscured in some modern editions that introduce scene breaks, for in so doing editors implicitly ignore the onstage presence of the scripted stage-sitters and its significance. Since the stage is only cleared (in the play-world) on four occasions, on the one hand correspondingly the act-breaks are particularly prominent, while on the other the constant presence of George and Nell (joined by Rafe) foregrounds the citizens as the narrative thread of the play; it is, in a sense, a blending of outdoor audience with indoor custom, not only at the level of theme but structure.

Q1613 does not provide indications of what editors signal as 'interludes', but it is clear where three of these fall. Before each interval (excepting the last) the text gives '*Boy danceth. Musicke*' (1/2, C4v) and '*Musicke*' (2/3, E3r; 3/4, G4v) – 3/4 adding '*Boy daunceth*' at the beginning of the new act – each of these followed by an exchange between the citizen and his wife prior to the entrance of the play-world characters. As has recently been suggested, Beaumont's play integrates its stage-sitter fictions so thoroughly that they are much more than the butt of an extended satirical joke (Smith 2012): the last of the four intervals brings to a climax the citizens' subversion of the socio-cultural milieu of the theatre-event in which they are, by its end, at its centre rather than on the periphery. Q signals the end of each act before the scripted stage-sitters comment on the action – except at 4/5, where 'Finis Act.4' (I2v) immediately precedes act 5, which some modern editors amend so that act 4 ends with the stage in the play-world cleared, whereupon the scripted stage-sitters comment, in what is by far the longest of these scripted sequences. We might infer that music (with a dancing boy) did not feature here, for Rafe is to 'dance the morrice' (I2r), which he then does. A popular rather than elite form of dance more suited to the amphitheatres, the morris symbolizes the citizens' usurpation of the Blackfriars (Smith 2012, 489–94); it is also a strident provocation to the gallants who may be obliged to forego their habitual behaviour during the interval. Thus the structure of the play and the centrality of the citizens are somewhat at odds with the conventional view that they are being mocked, and this might help explain Q1's reference to the play's failure. It is surely likely that the gallants resisted their usurpation by the citizen-characters – an ironically appropriate metatheatrical outcome.

In *The Staple of News* and *The Magnetic Lady* the formal structure is tighter: following their entrance in the Induction, the scripted stage-sitters are confined entirely to the intervals. This aligns with Jonson's principal purpose, which is to mock those who have the audacity to judge plays when they lack the understanding to do so. Both plays rehearse a familiar theme in Jonson's theatre, privileging the reader over the spectator, the former praised for taste and sensitivity, the latter condemned for their susceptibility to cheap spectacle. Correspondingly Jonson took special care when preparing texts for the press. The printed play demonstrates this in a striking intervention at 2/3 (placed directly after the second 'intermean', before act 3), the reader-playgoer opposition deployed as an exhortation 'To the Readers', inviting them to displace (and therefore correct) ex post facto the ignorant stage-sitters:

> In this following *Act*, the *Office* is open'd and shew'n to the *Prodigall* and his *Princesse Pecunia*, wherein the *allegory* and purpose of the *author* hath hitherto beene wholly mistaken, and so sinister an interpretation beene made, as if the soules

of most of the *Spectators* had liu'd in the eyes and eares of
these ridiculous Gossips that tattle between the *Acts*. But hee
prayes you thus to mend it. (E2v)

Tattle, Censure, Mirth, and Expectation are the four scripted gossips who in
the Induction follow the Prologue out of the tiring-house, rather than (like
Beaumont's *citizens*) entering from the audience to sit on the stage, for Mirth
refers to having been in the tiring-house (Aa2v). They then comment at
each of the intermeans. Jonson's satire on the emerging phenomenon of
news reportage, commodification, and reception activates a standard gender
trope so that the credulous consumers of this news are women, news
equated to gossip, opposed by art. Where Beaumont uses class to comment
on theatre culture, Jonson feints one way – the play framing the appetite for
news as effeminate – only to take another line: stage-sitting (ignorant and
erroneous) is gendered as female. In a line Jonson would reuse in *The New
Inn*, quoted previously, Mirth invokes Ovid (Parr 1988, 65n), declaring that
they have come 'to see and to be seen' (Aa2r); their interval dialogue,
correspondingly, is unselfconsciously frivolous, underpinning (yet also
undermining) 'Jonson's self-appointed mission to educate the public'
(Parr 1988, 23).

The intervention in the text at 2/3 suggests that the Prologue's appeal,
'Would you were come to heare, not see, a Play. / . . . He'ld [Jonson] haue
you wise / Much rather by your eares then by your eyes' (Aa3r), had fallen
on deaf ears since its first performance in 1626; indeed, apart from subsequently appearing at court it may not have been revived at all (Parr 1988,
49). The play gives the gossips free rein, but in so doing it cannot guarantee
that they condemn themselves out of their own mouths. Paradoxically, in
scripting these stage-sitters the dramatist acknowledges that he has little
actual control; irony, Janus-faced, looks both ways. At each intermean the
gossips demonstrate what Jonson regards as a not untypical ignorance, but
it is voiced nonetheless from a position of privilege (the text) *and* place (the
stage) that actual stage-sitters occupied. Jonson's twofold strategy, to
satirize the news as insubstantial and draw satirical portraits of stage-
sitters as equally ill-informed so that the play proper rises above this

froth, is a high-risk strategy, as the 2/3 address 'To the Readers' appears to acknowledge.

The Magnetic Lady suggests that this was a miscalculation because here the play adopts a more interventionist approach, ventriloquizing the author whose absence through illness otherwise takes the play out of his hands. Here Jonson takes aim at his sometime collaborator Inigo Jones, with whom he conducted a feud in the last years of his life. As critics have noted, the play has a valedictory air to it, but the scripted stage-sitting is concerned with the settling of scores. Whereas in Beaumont's play and *The Staple of News* the characters are all playgoers, in *The Magnetic Lady* two gentleman visitors, Probee and Damplay enter (implicitly from the tiring-house), and 'A BOY of the house, / *meets them*' (A2r). Damplay is a satirical portrait of Jones; Peter Happe conjectures that the Boy represents Richard Brome – by 1632 an established dramatist in his own right but in his youth a servant of some sort to Jonson – whose function is to present Jonson's own voice and views on drama (Happé 2000, 220–2). Again, the point of this fiction is correction of error, but here the dramatist leaves less to chance, and therefore places considerable emphasis, and indeed pressure, on its use of the interval, since it is here that the play's adherence to classical modalities is explained and defended, with Jones the butt of Jonson's satire – thus killing two birds with one stone.

Or so Jonson hoped. For all that these plays are formally sophisticated and innovative, none seems to have been a success on the stage. Walter Burre, the publisher of Beaumont's play, expresses regret for its '*expos[ure] to the wide[r] world, who for want of iudgement, or not vnderstanding the priuy marke of* Ironie *about it . . . vtterly reiected it*' (Q1, A2r). The inserted paratextual material in *The Staple of News* at 2/3 does not suggest the play was a success on stage (Bentley 1941–68, IV: 630; Parr 1988, 49), though it accords with his views on stage-sitters. His use of the act-time in *The Magnetic Lady* to attack Inigo Jones through dialogue between Boy and Damplay backfired when Jones himself attended a performance and, turning the tables, like Damplay 'did indeed ridicule the play' from the audience (Happé 2000, 12), though whether this exchange took place on the stage itself is a nice question; another antagonist, Alexander Gill, penned a poem attacking Jonson and his play (Happé 2000, 215–17).

The reasons for the apparent failure of these plays are no doubt complex. But that they have one feature in common does raise a practical question. How was this scripted material actually performed, when (customarily) music played, candles were tended, and, crucially, the *actual* stage-sitters presumably expected to behave as they wished? Scripting fictional stage-sitters must have been perceived as a direct challenge by playgoers: it would seem unlikely that gallants who paid extra partly to exhibit behaviour of which some playmakers (notably Jonson) disapproved would meekly allow themselves to be muted in this way. In effect Beaumont and Jonson eliminate the interval temporally. Something had to give. At the very least it seems unlikely that stage-sitters who took advantage of the act-time in a play where the stage was cleared one day would alter that behaviour the next. And yet there is another factor to consider. It was the interval that made the stage-sitters' ostentatious display possible, and presumably their antics were tolerated by other playgoers only because the play had paused; yet stage-sitters might be seen in another light, as interfering with the play and with the wider audience's enjoyment. The tensions at Salisbury Court that came to a head in 1639 were not confined to that venue, and an argument at the Blackfriars in the year that *The Magnetic Lady* was staged which led to a lord standing on the stage drawing his sword and only narrowly missing a disgruntled spectator whose view he had blocked (Gurr 2004, 288) shows that playmakers were not alone in their frustrations with audience behaviour. Above all, however, that we lack more examples of the innovation we find in these three plays suggests that what scholars have praised as metatheatre came up against the harsh facts of indoor playmaking – and stage-sitting. The scripting of act-time business *with dialogue* does indeed suggest that 'the Intermeans replaced the customary musical interludes' (Parr 1988, 152n), but more significantly it threatened to deprive stage-sitters of their voice, as well as their place.

4 Amphitheatre < > Hall

Acting companies were accustomed to operating in diverse conditions. On the road they had to be flexible; in the capital, too. The Newington Butts playhouse – where Henslowe records a brief Admiral's-Chamberlain's tenure in June 1594 (Foakes 2002, 21–2) – may have been an indoor theatre

(Johnson 2018, 46), the royal palaces hosted performances indoors, and both the Bell and Cross Keys inns on Gracious Street, which flourished into the 1590s, may also have used large rooms, rather than inn-yards, as it seems was universally the case in taverns in the 1540s (Kathman 2009, 163, 154). If Cross Keys was an indoor venue, as the newly formed Chamberlain's Men petition to use it in the winter of 1594 would seem to indicate, the company must have felt they could stage their amphitheatre repertory there. Yet surprisingly little scholarship has explored the practicalities of this inter-space mobility. Admittedly, so many plays are lost that statements of a general nature can only be provisional: thus, it may or may not be representative of this mostly lost corpus that very few texts register the habitual movement between venue types there undoubtedly was. The signal trace of such a trajectory is the interval.

4.1 Tracing Conversion

Until the King's Men began playing at the Blackfriars a decade into the new century the adult companies were essentially 'amphitheatre companies', accustomed to playing outdoors, able to adapt to indoor conditions as required. By chance some outdoor plays had 'readymade' act-breaks – points in the text where the stage was (already) conveniently cleared – which made calculations relatively straightforward, and no doubt sometimes gave the offstage 'continuity text' new significance. But in such cases, number unknown, adaptation left no traces – especially where a printed play registers essentially only one iteration, as is the situation with the vast majority of the surviving corpus. For example, the title page of *The Two Maids of More-Clacke* (Q1609) proclaims that it was 'Played by the Children of the Kings Maiesties Reuels', whose Whitefriars operation lasts for a mere nine months in 1607–1608. However, the play was a self-penned vehicle for Robert Armin's expertise as a clown, written a decade earlier (prior to his joining the Chamberlain's Men as Will Kempe's replacement). The play 'may have been refurbished for a Whitefriars performance' (Bly 2000, 48), but if so it is curious that Q is undivided, which points to its amphitheatre origins. If Q was used as the basis for an indoor performance, the Whitefriars company would have had to locate four points where act-breaks could be inserted. More likely, perhaps, another text was used, whose relationship to Q is irretrievable. In this case Q represents a previous iteration, the title-page attribution a new label on an old text.

But there are extant texts where the outdoor > indoor and (less commonly) indoor > outdoor process *is* detectable. While in the corpus of printed drama examples are few, the comparatively small number of manuscript witnesses – playhouse plots and playbooks – is rich in evidence. In both cases textual revision or emendation may be traced back to the significance of the interval as distinguishing feature. The wider context is that these documents register the rise of adult indoor playmaking later in the period.

4.2 The Manuscript Interval

The provenance of these documents is by no means settled, but a number of them illustrate the process as well as outcome of outdoor > indoor conversion, ruling out some hypotheses and advancing others. The marking of intervals is a telltale sign of how writers proposed, and bookkeepers disposed.

Of the seven surviving plots, one stands out. Not because in naming one 'Burbage' among its actors *The Dead Man's Fortune* presents scholars with a puzzle: how might this British Library text (Ms. Add.10449, f.1), having passed into the hands of George Steevens in the 18th century, be linked to the Chamberlain's/King's Men, and even to Dulwich College, and thus to Edward Alleyn? As Tiffany Stern points out, 'the companies and theatres that used the[se] plots, and the periods of time from which the plots date, are all open to debate' (Stern 2009, 203). For present purposes these issues are secondary to (but affected by) a feature that distinguishes '<T>he plotte of the deade mans fo^{r}tune' from the other six: the marking of act-breaks.

Like the other extant plots designed for use within the tiring-house and consisting of a single sheet of paper affixed to a post so it could be consulted easily, *The Dead Man's Fortune* uses horizontal and vertical lines to create boxes, each apparently corresponding to a unit of action, rather than designating a scene as such (Greg 1931, I: 97). To this visual structure, representing in skeletal form the working practices of the amphitheatre, has been added material that moves this plot into another register. Four act-breaks are rendered (in all but one instance, the last) thus '-x-x-x-x-x-x-x-x-x-x', and directly alongside each in the left-hand margin appears the direction 'musique'. Greg identified two hands, not one, the second scribe adding the act-break and marginal directions for music, as well as an additional scene (squeezed into blank space in the margin) that would begin the now-designated act 5 (Greg 1931, I: 96–7, 103). From this he deduced, oddly, that 'although the actual performance was divided into acts, there may have been no indication of this in the Book' (Greg 1931, I: 97). These paleographical findings tell a different story.

'<T>he plotte of the deade mans fo^rtune' is a palimpsestic record of adaptation. After the first scribe (Hand A) had prepared the plot from the manuscript given to him, at some point subsequently a decision was taken to convert it for performance indoors. The nature of these plots is that few exits are marked, and not all the horizontal lines indicate a cleared stage. Hand B had to identify four appropriate places to break the action; the play ends with the subplot characters effecting the denouement – 'Enter the panteloun & causeth the / cheste or truncke to be brought forth' – and it may not be coincidental that he decided that each of the acts would close with a subplot scene. This process was further complicated by the insertion of the additional scene, but at any rate Hand B seems to have been able to marry a practical requirement (the candle-tending, which presumably he calculated with the aid of the manuscript from which the plot was prepared) with an aesthetic sensitivity that gave the indoor version a specific structural pattern. He also added 'musique', code for the interval. If such information in plots is not cued as such (Stern 2009, 214), there can be no doubt here that as acts 1–4 ended the music *was* cued, and not only for the audience: within the tiring-house these four aural events served as signals of the play's progress.

Greg thought it most likely that, originally, the added scene had been an accidental omission by Hand A (Greg 1931, 95, 98). Conversely, in Scott McMillin's view it 'looks like a late insertion intended to serve a pragmatic theatrical purpose'; he argues that '[w]ithout the insertion, the sub-plot actors would have appeared in the scene preceding the conclusion. . . . With the insertion . . . [they] would have gained time to dress for their doubled roles in the conclusion' (McMillin 1973, 238). In other words, it was realized that some of the actors in the subplot would be needed for the long scene where the king enters and as many as sixteen actors are needed on stage at the same time (Bradley 1992, 95). But if the additional scene was part of a new design, its purpose was not to solve the kind of problem McMillin identifies because the 4/5 act-break does that.

Identification of the other actors named in the plot does not help establish either the company behind it or the date(s), but Burbage's name also features in another of the surviving plots, *The Seven Deadly Sins*. Although traditionally dated to the early 1590s, a strong case has been made for its belonging to the Chamberlain's Men, for whom Burbage of course was a leading member, in 1597–1598 (Kathman 2004, 2011), and circumstantial evidence might support a similar argument here. The company failed in its attempt to secure permission to perform at Cross Keys, and two years later in 1596, its Blackfriars plan was scuppered by the opposition of local residents. Nevertheless, this plot may represent the earliest firm evidence of that history indoors, at some point in the 1590s. This might have been at court or the Inns of Court (Taylor 1993, 28–29), but the hole in the document points to tiring-house practice (Hirrel 2010, 179n); an earlier date, in the 'mid-1580s', before the Chamberlain's Men were formed, has also been suggested (Taylor 1993, 13). Either way, the revised plot points inexorably towards some kind of indoor staging.

Of the surviving playbooks (holograph or scribal), a number show signs of revision for indoor performance. Excepting the amphitheatre play *Sir Thomas More*, they are divided into acts (and, sometimes, scenes), most dating (it follows) from later in the period. Thus eight of them, all composed for performance indoors – at the Phoenix (*The Two Noble Ladies, The Welsh Ambassador, The Parliament of Love, The Captives*); for Salisbury Court (*The Lady Mother, The Wasp*); and at an unidentified indoor venue (*The Faithful Friends, The Launching of the Mary*) – are not my concern here; similarly, *Charlemagne*, perhaps by Chapman, is divided into acts with directions for music and, dating to the early 17th century, it is almost certainly a children's play. *Sir Thomas More* and *John a Kent and John a Cumber*, wholly or partly in the hand of Anthony Munday, are both amphitheatre plays, neither of which bears the traces of revival. *John a Kent* (which may be the same play as *The Wise Man of West Chester*), dates from 1590x96 (the last digit is unclear), and its divisions are wholly classical in origin, ignored if this is the play the Admiral's Men staged at the Rose in 1594–1597. Of rather more interest are several that, like the plot for *The Dead Man's Fortune*, suggest a later (re)iteration.

If *Thomas of Woodstock* was also an amphitheatre play revived indoors (Long 1999, 421–3), then its act-division was either 'classical' (as with *John a Kent*) or added later, when intervals were needed; conversely, if this is a 17th-century play (Jackson 2001, 23; Egan 2011, 381), then the act markings may have been original. The marginal note for 'A bed', which William Long takes as *not* signalling the readying of a stage property (Long 1985, 108–9) appears just before an act-break, so it would seem to have a practical purpose after all (Egan 2011, 382). The question remains open. We can be rather more certain about two plays that certainly were written for the amphitheatre, *Edmund Ironside* and *John of Bordeaux*, both of which were revived in the 1630s, and thus required act-breaks; of the former it is most likely that act-breaks were added then (Long 1999, 424).

This process is also traceable in several King's Men's plays. Three play-books are in the hand of Edward Knight (who became the company book-keeper sometime after 1616 [Ioppolo 2012, xiii]): *The Honest Man's Fortune*; *The Soddered Citizen*; and *Believe As You List*, Philip Massinger, having replaced John Fletcher around 1625 as the troupe's principal writer. *The Honest Man's Fortune* was staged in 1613 by Lady Elizabeth's Men – presumably at the Whitefriars rather than the Swan, since it has an LRE-interval at 4/5 – before being relicensed in 1625 for the King's Men. When it was printed in the Beaumont and Fletcher Folio (1647) it included a scene and other material not present in the MS. Structurally insignificant and 'easily detachable' (Ioppolo 2012, xxi), the additions (whoever made them) seem to be artistic. *The Soddered Citizen*, however, is a different matter. Here it is noteworthy that Knight saw fit to partly restructure John Clavell's play, finding fault with the authorial act-breaks: he moves the opening scene of the final act to the end of act 4, the 4/5 interval thus taking place one scene later. While he conscientiously renumbers the scenes in act 5 (Greg 1955, 144), his prime concern is with the placing of the interval. That Clavell was an amateur playwright is likely a factor in the problems Knight identified.

The holograph *Believe as You List* provides a helpful comparator. Clearly the dramatist knew he was writing for the Blackfriars – that the act lengths would work indoors (there being no such constraint if the play was staged at the Globe). What is interesting is Knight's treatment of the MS he received. Long states that the bookkeeper 'deletes all Massinger's act and scene divisions and adds his own: he marks the beginning of each act with a short line to the exact beginning line in the text' (Long 1999, 430), and Martin White suggests that Knight 'marked the act divisions and rearranged the text to suit his own practical preferences' (White 2018, 196). In fact, while Knight *does* cross out most of the *scene* breaks, it is more accurate to say that after deleting the act-divisions he reinstates them, using his own form of notation. Knight concurs with Massinger's act-divisions, and reinforces them. (As noted previously, at two of these he marks the interval 'Long'.) Thus, as Knight recognized, this professional playwright was fully cognizant of theatre practicalities, unlike his amateur counterpart, Clavell, whose notion of act-division perhaps owed more to 'classical' notions.

4.3 Print Traces: Outdoor > Indoor

Conversion is also evident in plays that exist in more than one version. Two examples in the Shakespeare canon, each first printed in quarto and subsequently in folio, offer a sub-narrative of the company's trajectory from an amphitheatre operation (performing indoors on occasion) to a dual-theatre company operating at the Globe and Blackfriars in parallel, as well as at court.

4.3.1 A Midsummer Night's Dream

Scholars have long been aware of a crux in the 1623 folio text, which might have prompted further investigation. While editors note the stage business at 3/4 and endorse F's act-divisions, it has been left at that.

In the amphitheatre, when the four lovers are in the wood and drugged by Puck, they fall asleep on the stage, and he exits; subsequently Titania and the 'translated' Bottom enter, and the lovers awaken. At no point is the stage cleared. So much for Q1-2 (1600, 1619). In F, after Puck's exit, an act-break is inserted, following a new sd: '*They sleepe all the Act*' (TLN1507). That is, during the act-time the lovers remain on stage, asleep. There are at least two ways of interpreting this crux. On the surface, breaking into the continuous sequence here was not ideal: it may well be that because the action between 2/3 and this point already amounted to almost 700 lines (TLN813-1507) there was no other option – the next opportunity (when the stage is cleared) would be another 40, 50, or more than 200 lines later. Generally, the evidence examined for this Element suggests that players preferred not to cut amphitheatre texts, opting instead for least-worst solutions to make the original text work indoors. Alternatively – or additionally – it may be that the company saw a positive in this problem. Indoors, the music and dancing boy provided a suitable accompaniment to suggest a state of sleep – and perhaps did double duty for the continuing nightmare, offstage, of Bottom with his ass's head – who enters with Titania at the beginning of act 4. The lovers remaining on stage was thus both perfectly logical and in keeping with the flexibility the interval offered. Here, at any rate, the King's Men effectively maintained the play's amphitheatre staging indoors, minimising disruption to either text or performance tradition, and augmenting the effect with the interval music.

The ease with which outdoor design segues into indoor practice is echoed in editorial treatment of the relationship between Q and F texts. Perhaps the lack of fuss over F's additional sd at TLN1507 is partly explained by a similar scenario at 2/3, but for which F supplies no new sd. Here, Titania is lulled to sleep, drugged, to the singing of the fairies (TLN660-76); she remains there, and upon his entry is addressed by Oberon: 'What thou seest when thou dost wake, / Doe it for thy true Loue take' (TLN678-79). Successively the four lovers enter, and then exit; the Queen of the Fairies remains asleep on stage, which in F spans the 2/3 act-break, foreshadowing 3/4. Inserting intervals in *A Midsummer Night's Dream* is at once complicated by the lack of stage clearance and simplified by the play-world scenario.

4.3.2 Titus Andronicus

Q1-3 (1594, 1600, and 1611) convey the play's outdoor provenance, but F's imposition of act-breaks illustrates how an old play might be reshaped for new staging requirements. The opening sequence, up to the point where the stage is first cleared, is a long one – too long, evidently, for the candles to be relied on. Q1-3 signals '*Exeunt. / sound Trumpets, Manet Moore*' (C2r). Saturninus and Tamora, with her two surviving sons Chiron and Demetrius, Marcus and Titus with two of his sons, and Bassianus and Lavinia, all exit here. Aaron, remaining, delivers a soliloquy, the function of which in part is to allow Chiron and Demetrius to re-enter, and to be primed for the revenge they will enact in the hunting sequence, following the exit of these three characters. It is at this point that – stage cleared, location changing – an act-break would make most sense, as editors since the 18th century have recognised. Indeed, an agent in the printing house intent on imposing a classical five-act structure could readily have done so, and this would have been *easier* than what actually transpired.

Instead, in the 1623 text the designated first act ends earlier, just before Aaron delivers his soliloquy. F reads '*Exeunt*', followed by '*Actus Secunda*', placed within two horizontal lines, and then '*Flourish. Enter Aaron alone*' (TLN552-54). Placing the interval here allows Aaron to reappear immediately. It is a neat solution to the candle issue, but has not been understood as such by scholars (from Johnson onwards). Stanley Wells, for example, approaches the matter from a purely editorial perspective: should an editor follow Q or F, he ponders, recognizing that a 'more logical procedure [than adopting F's reading] would have been to abandon the act and scene break altogether. This, of course, entails the inconvenience of sabotaging the conventional system of reference' (Wells 1979, 107). Thus for editors who wish to open up questions of act- and/or scene-division to scrutiny their hands are tied. Wells acknowledges that 'there are grounds for supposing that the Folio represents, not merely a printing-house imposition upon the text, but a change in staging after the play had been produced' (Wells 1979, 108). However, while he connects the LRE with act-breaks, the further move – technology-determined intervals – is not made.

F provides strong evidence for the play's later theatrical provenance, and confirmation is found later in the text. This collaboration with George Peele may date from as early as 1588 or more probably around 1591–1592; evidently it was long considered part of the company's repertory, its appearance in quarto three times pointing to its longevity. At some point it was revised. The most significant difference between F and its predecessors is the 'fly scene'. The Norton editor considers this addition to be part of a revision in 1594 (Maus 1997, 378), though the printing of the three quartos (one that very year) without this scene is therefore problematic. On the basis that, like Jonson's additions to *The Spanish Tragedy* in c.1597–1602 (appearing in the 1602 quarto), the protagonist's madness is accentuated, another editor argues for a date around this time (Bate 1995, 118). Here, too, its absence in print until 1623 is awkward. Most recently, Thomas Middleton's authorship has been proposed, sometime after 1608 (Taylor and Duhaime 2017). What is key is its structural significance. As with the interpolated act-division foreshortening the opening scene, really the best explanation for its presence is that it occurred when the play was staged indoors.

In Q1-3, after Titus is tricked by Aaron into cutting off his own hand, the stage is cleared, all bar Lucius, who delivers a soliloquy before exiting, his purpose to go into exile and raise an army of Goths against Rome; the location shifting, Lucius's son and Lavinia then enter, followed by Titus and Marcus. It is between these two sequences that the additional scene appears (TLN1451-1539). Jonathan Bate remarks that this scene 'requires a group of characters to go offstage and come straight back, something that Shakespeare nearly always avoided' (Bate 1997, 117–18), but he is thinking of the LRE and *outdoor* performance. In a recent edition of the play Alan Hughes ponders whether 'playhouse custom had changed … [that] an interval was inserted between Acts 3 and 4' (Hughes 2006, 48; qtd. in Dutton 2016, 260). That must be so. The new scene (designated 3.2 in modern editions) brings the third act to a close, but there is no LRE problem, since an interval allows for Titus and Marcus's exit and re-entrance either side of 3/4.

In fact, structurally the new scene can *only* make sense in an indoor context, since it requires an act-break to make it work. W.W. Greg was on the right lines when he suggested that were it not for the additional scene the third act would be very short, but he erred in supposing that the scene predated the division of the play into acts (Greg 1955, 204–5; quoted in Bate 1995, 118). The placing of the new scene before rather than after the interval eliminated the LRE problem it would otherwise present, and of course provided an opportunity to trim the candles; it also made possible the use of both flanking doors, 'severally', which the sequence suggests may have been the case (Bate 1995, 210n). It seems clear, then, that the fly-killing scene was added to the play for staging indoors, as the introduction of act-breaks also indicates; attributing the new scene to Shakespeare may well point to a court production (Dutton 2016, 260), or to the company's indoor theatre, after 1608, perhaps by another playwright (Taylor and Duhaime 2017).

4.4 Print Traces: Indoor > Outdoor

Given the historical current, into which the influence of the resurgent children's theatre flowed, it is not surprising that the dominant shift was amphitheatre > hall. But occasionally plays did move in the other direction. As with outdoor > indoor conversion, there might be additions, but going the other way was principally a matter of subtraction: out went the intervals and the music; and if an indoor play used the LRE-interval device, this necessitated substantial alterations.

4.4.1 The Malcontent

In 1604 the King's Men acquired (in dubious circumstances) Marston's play, which had been written for and performed by the Children of the Queen's Revels, operating at the Blackfriars; it must have been successful there, not only to appeal to the King's Men but because it would be printed three times that year. The differences between these texts (introduced in Q3) offer a snapshot of how a company went about converting an indoor play for the amphitheatre.

Q3 is somewhat longer than its two predecessors. The title page proclaims that this version has been 'Augmented by *Marston.* / With the Additions played by the Kings Maiesties Servants. / Written by *Ihon Webster*'; the Induction indicates that the children's *Malcontent* was too short for outdoor performance, hence the need for additions which (the Induction aside) amount to some 447 lines (Hunter 1975, xlviii), adding almost 25 per cent to the original play. But of course the company faced a practical issue of another order, namely that at the Globe there would be neither intervals nor musical framing. Comparing the Q1-2 texts with Q3 shows clearly that some of this new material was designed to address this problem. But even in its revised state, the original act-time business at 1/2 poses questions about quite how this sequence was accommodated at the Globe. Whoever was responsible for the additions in acts 1–5, the company seems to have believed that this material could still work, but in a different way.

Q3 is best characterized as consisting of 'additions', rather than *revision*. For the Globe what was required was a structural adjustment, not wholesale changes relating to plot or characterization; no characters are eliminated or amalgamated, and only one newly introduced (Passarello, who accounts for around 25 per cent of the new lines [Hunter 1975, xlix]). Q3 features 11 new chunks of text, all but two of which are incorporated into extant scenes. Two additional sections were added to what modern editions designate 1.3, one each to 1.4, 1.8, 2.3, 3.1, and all but one scene of the final act received new material: 5.1–5.4, and 5.6. Editors have focused on the content rather than the form, but the two entirely new scenes do not have a 'literary' or plot function but a structural one. The children's *Malcontent* exploited the interval to circumvent the LRE at 1/2, which also features an act-time dumb show, and at 4/5: correspondingly it is at these points that the King's Men had to devise and insert two entirely new scenes (1.8 and 5.1) so that Mendoza and Malevole respectively do not exit and re-enter immediately. Had Marston not used the interval in this way in the original Blackfriars play there would have been no need for these additional scenes.

The King's Men version does not conceal its performance history, however – far from it, boasting of the play's origins and explicitly drawing attention to the differences between indoor and outdoor practices. William Sly enters, intent on watching the play as a stage-sitter: in response to the tireman's remark, 'Sir, the gentlemen will be angry if you sit there', he asks 'Why? We may sit upon the stage at the private house' (Ind.1–2). 'W. Sly', as Q3 styles him, is an actor: he appears here as a fictionalized version of himself – 'thou tookest me for one of the players' (Ind.4–5) – entering as he does from the tiring house (as a stage-sitter would), and then asking: 'Where's Harry Condell, Dick Burbage, and Will Sly?' (Ind.11–12). This knockabout stuff frames the play *congruously* as the indoor-outdoor hybrid it was. If Q3's preservation of the 1/2 act-time business is an accurate record of the Globe's rendering of the play then the King's Men incorporated Marston's original design; but if so, the act-time sequence at Blackfriars was transformed into a prefatory dumb show that, once concluded, gives way to Mendoza's soliloquy:

> *Enter Mendoza with a Sconce, to observe* Fernezes *entrance, who whilest the Act is playing* : *Enter vnbraced two pages before him with lights, is met by* Maquerrelle *and conuayed. The pages are sent away.*

(Q3, C4v)

This scenario is only made possible by the inserted scene (1.8) which enables Mendoza to exit, re-enter, witness the dumb show, deliver his soliloquy, and exit again. The incorporation of the original interval business as a dumb show is surely less powerful than Marston's signature scripting of the act-time, but once again we can see that playmakers were reluctant to make radical changes to plays they needed to adapt to fit performance conditions. They made the extant text work. In the Induction, in response to Sly's query about the play belonging to another company, Condell's's oft-quoted reply alludes to the seeming theft of a King's Men play by the children's company, and Burbage/'Burbage' summarises the changes made by the adults:

Cun: Why not Maleuole in folio with vs, as Ieronimo in de-Cimo sexto with them. They taught vs a name for our play, wee call it *One for another.*
Sly: What are your additions?
Bur: Sooth not greatly needefull, only as your sallet to your greate feast, to entertaine a little more time, and to abridge the not-received custom of musicke in our Theater. (Q3, A4r)

Burbage's culinary metaphor obscures the extent and significance of the structural alternations noted earlier; but it is the reference to the 'custom of music' at the Blackfriars that scholars have focused on, noting that music was both more sophisticated and important to the performance event than it was at the Globe – hence the need to 'abridge' the music. Unfortunately, neither Q1 nor Q2 preserves the music or instruments that featured at the Blackfriars so a comparison is not possible. But it is worth noting what is elided here: it was the interval that both made possible and required music, giving indoor performance its particular distinctiveness. Coming three years before *The Knight of the Burning Pestle* would poke fun at amphitheatre playgoers, the King's Men mock-mocked the indoor theatre they envied and would secure a few years later.

5 The Globe < > Blackfriars Effect

The King's Men's takeover of the Blackfriars in 1608 complicated the company's operations, though not immediately. The debate over how the two playhouses were used pivots on the interval, and the traces it has left.

There are two main (and one subsidiary) possibilities: (i) as per Bentley, the King's Men ran two distinct repertories over three decades, up to the general closure of the theatres; (ii) conversely, the company operated a dual-playhouse/single repertory strategy, in effect maintaining a single bank of malleable plays; (iii) the King's Men designed and managed a hybrid repertory, consisting of Globe-only, Blackfriars-only, and 'dual-code' plays.

Collating interval-related information provides a form- rather than content-based picture of how the King's Men appear to have operated from as early as the second decade of the 17th century onwards. As unfortunate as the 1613 Globe fire was, the company's response is a helpful pointer, for its rebuilding demonstrates that (i) the sharers did not feel that their amphitheatre had been superseded by the Blackfriars; (ii) its strategy for 1610–1613 (as it turned out) had been deemed a success; and therefore (iii) perhaps most significantly that the longer term strategy was precisely that the company would continue to operate in two, distinct venues: the Globe, already old in 1613, was in 1614 key – *still* – to the company's long-term plans. Indeed, it has been argued that the Globe was the more important venue, up to 1619 and even 1625 (Knutson 2002, 116). From this it might follow that the innovation of c.1610–1613 had provided the basis for a long-term repertory management plan.

As the Appendix sets out, of the plays composed or acquired over a thirty-year period, the title pages of only four designate the plays as staged at the Globe alone. Only a slightly higher number, six, were on this authority staged at both theatres, while the majority, forty-one, are flagged as Blackfriars plays. This crude data might initially support Bentley's contention that the older, amphitheatre repertory kept the Globe going through these years, the company putting its resources for commissioning new plays principally into its indoor venue. However, half of this total of plays appeared in folio, and thus on the basis of venue (non-)attribution alone they may have appeared at either theatre, or both. Clearly title-page information is insufficient on its own, not least when it is relevant to only just over half of the repertory. Small wonder that scholars, perhaps rightly suspicious of convenient binaries, have discerned similarity rather than difference in this cohort of plays, which of course helps underwrite the prevailing view that this most successful of companies moved effortlessly between venue types – amphitheatre, indoor playhouse, and court. Indeed, surviving court records where the chosen play is named do themselves put rather a dent in the low/high culture model that is still used to distinguish between the enduring outdoor venues in the liberties and their upmarket counterparts established inside the walls in the fashionable west of the city.

But when this title-page data is combined with LRE information the question of provenance and repertory management shifts to staging practicalities. In fifty-nine texts, in one or more instances a character exits and re-enters, across act-breaks; this correlates as follows with the title-page claims. A total of 33 plays share both characteristics, and this figure breaks down thus: Globe: 1; Blackfriars: 28; Globe and Blackfriars: 4. What is most striking but least surprising is that it is predominantly (85 per cent) those designated exclusively Blackfriars plays that illustrate this pattern. This data bears out the general argument in the preceding pages, that dramatists exploited the interval for practical purposes; still, there remains the puzzle of the solitary play in this category that its title page associates with the Globe, as well as four others linked to both venues.

The number of Globe-only plays, as designated by the title page, is suspiciously small (four), though any of the more than twenty non-LRE plays in collections could have been staged there without obvious difficulty (as might Blackfriars-designated, non-LRE plays, some twenty-three in total). Only one of the four, Massinger's *The Unnatural Combat* (1624) presents a problem for amphitheatre production, at 2/3. Q1639 has Beaufort Senior entering at the beginning of act 3, despite the fact that he also appears at the end of the previous act. However, with no exit signalled, it is possible for him to do so just before the end of act 2, on his line declaring to another character that he will expect him. Alternatively, Q (but not its title page) registers indoor performance; *or,* by this time the Globe had adopted intervals. For, in six plays designated Globe *and* Blackfriars, the act-time is exploited to thwart the LRE. Here an apparent duality may also point to act-breaks at the Globe, but it may also be that, as with the case of *Satiromastix,* the printed text records a particular phase of the play's performance history. Examination of the earliest of these six Globe and Blackfriars plays provides an illustration of a possible scenario that may help explain such 'duality'.

5.0.1 The Duchess of Malfi

Q1623, printed a decade after *The Duchess of Malfi* was first staged, contains two pieces of significant information on its title page. It adver- tises the play '*As it was Presented priuately, at the Black- / friars; and publicly at the Globe, By the* / Kings Maiesties Seruants'. Taken at face value this lends support to the view that the company staged at least some of its plays at both venues. But this possibility has to be evaluated in terms of the additional claim that Q presents 'The perfect and exact Coppy, with diuerse / *things Printed, that the length of the Play would* / not beare in the Presentment'. One reading of this is that it is a publisher's puff to make the quarto more attractive to readers. That the statement is then followed with 'VVritten by *John Webster*' invites the potential buyer to infer that the claim is authorial. Another possible interpretation is that Webster is distinguishing between the play and the (longer) 'poem', which represents not the play as performed but the 'perfect and exact Coppy' of the dramatist's text for the *reader* (Erne 2003, 169). But these two statements, taken together, must be interrogated alongside a feature of the text itself.

Leaving aside the second statement for a moment, the first encounters a familiar staging issue when we examine Q. Whatever the 'Presentment' entailed, Q indicates that Webster made use of the interval for LRE purposes. Towards the end of act 3 the duchess and Cariola are on stage and Bosola enters, with guards. Q indicates that they all exit together. Yet at the beginning of act 4 Bosola enters with Ferdinand: unproblematic at the Blackfriars, of course, but not at the Globe. If the play was staged both indoors and outdoors, Q does not represent the play as staged at the latter. If the second statement does distinguish between what was staged and what is present, in the printed text, then Q is closer to the Blackfriars version than it is to the Globe's.

It may be that Webster wrote *The Duchess of Malfi* specifically for indoor conditions, and it was the company's decision to stage it outdoors as well (as the direction of travel on the title page indicates): in which case the 3/4 exit/re-entry of Bosola had to be accommodated in some way. Act 3 ends with the duchess telling Bosola a story; an exit for him before the end of the tale is implausible because Bosola's purpose is to take her to her 'pallace' (Q1623, H4r), and three lines from the end of the scene she acquiesces: 'But come: whether you please' (H4v). At the Globe a joint exit closing the scene would enable the succeeding scene to begin smoothly, yet something must have been done to avoid the re-entry at the beginning of act 4, which begins with Ferdinand's enquiry to Bosola, 'How doth our sister Dutchesse beare herselfe / In her imprisonment?' (I1r). Q is already long at around 3,000 lines, so an additional scene interceding here is unlikely, and its omission from the apparently longer, printed text proclaiming the author's apparent preferences would make little sense. Since the problem is Bosola, an alternative solution would be to omit the sequence where he enters with the guards (regardless of the weakening of the play this would entail). All this is speculation, but the 3/4 interval means that whatever it is that Q represents, the Blackfriars and Globe scripts surely differed at this point in the play – unless, of course, Q represents the staging at both theatres after all, with intervals at the Globe, as the play in this form required.

5.1 Globe < Interval > Blackfriars

Overall, what this data shows is that there is a growth in the use of the LRE-interval over the course of the thirty years the King's Men operated in two theatres. (Of the 59 plays that deploy it, 25 use it more than once – Massinger's *The Emperor of the East* at each act-break.) Again, using these 101 texts, and breaking the period down into roughly five-year segments (1609–1614; 1615–1620; 1621–1626; 1627–1632; 1633–1638; 1639–1642), the use of the device in plays measured against the total number of texts reads: 7/15; 14/22; 8/16; 7/16: 15/22; 8/10. It was in the company's economic interests to be able to switch plays between venues (Knutson 2006), rather than restrict its room for manoeuvre, since it would not need to commission, pay for, and rehearse as many plays if it doubled up. It is difficult to resist the conclusion that the logic of a dual playhouse strategy, which the rebuilding of the Globe reinforced, led to a splicing together of stage practices, even if some amphitheatre plays remained Globe staples and other, indoor plays, for whatever reason did not cross the Thames. That the title page of *The Emperor of the East* (1631), with its use of the interval-LRE device at 1/2, 2/3, 3/4, and 4/5 allocates the play to both playhouses is not otherwise readily fathomable; similarly, apart from Webster's play discussed earlier, Brome's *The Northern Lass* (1629) and Heywood's *A Challenge for Beauty* (1634) also fall into this category. Perhaps, by the time of the printing of *The Duchess of Malfi* (1623), the Globe had adopted intervals, or the printed texts recorded the indoor iterations only.

Data analysis will not be a perfect fit for any hypothesis due to the varied nature of textual production. This evidence – such as it is – provides a general impression rather than allowing firm conclusions to be drawn. But what is clear is that the fundamental questions surrounding the company's repertory management revolve around the structure of performance. As shown previously, movement between theatre types often required intervention. However important the Globe was to the King's Men, the future lay indoors, inside the city walls; this may not have been clear in 1608 (since it seems not to have been in 1613–1614), but Beeston's Cockpit venture in 1616, the opening of Salisbury Court in 1629 and Cockpit-in-Court in 1629–1630 – and perhaps even, above all, the court's favouring of the company throughout this period – may all have urged the King's Men to regard Blackfriars and its practices as central to its identity. Whether the Globe, correspondingly, was brought into a kind of alignment with Blackfriars, adopting its intervals as it seems to have done with its music – two aspects of indoor performance that are intertwined, of course, so logically it would make sense that the desire to exploit the reputation of the children's theatre for musical accomplishment capitalised on the feature that accentuated the role of music in theatrical presentation – this debate situates the plays of the company's chief playwright at the heart of the matter. If Bentley is right, then Shakespeare's old, amphitheatre plays remained at the Globe. But the textual situation of the Shakespeare canon that has driven three centuries of scholarship sits no more easily with that proposition than with any other. The question of how the King's Men managed their playhouses inevitably leads to interrogation of the Shakespearean texts that appeared in print some fifteen years after the Blackfriars was taken over.

5.2 The Shakespearean Text

Shakespeare wrote almost exclusively for the outdoor playhouse: had James Burbage's attempt to secure the Blackfriars for the Chamberlain's Men in 1596 succeeded it would surely have been otherwise. The printing of the plays in his lifetime reflected this. Not until 1622 would a quarto (*Othello*) appear with act and scene divisions, but a year later the First Folio presented a more complicated (and arguably more accurate) picture of their performance history.

John Heminges and Henry Condell brought together thirty-six plays (including collaborations) under one roof in 1623, omitting *Pericles* and *Two Noble Kinsmen*. Only six of these follow the quarto 'precedent' in being undivided: *2 and 3 Henry VI, Troilus and Cressida, Romeo and Juliet, Timon of Athens*, and *Antony and Cleopatra* (the latter two unavailable prior to 1623). Of the remaining thirty, fully or partially* divided, sixteen appeared in print for the first time: *The Tempest, The Two Gentlemen of Verona, Measure for Measure, The Comedy of Errors*, *As You like It, The Taming of the Shrew, All's Well That Ends Well, Twelfth Night, The Winter's Tale, King John, 1 Henry VI, Henry VIII, Coriolanus, Julius Caesar, Macbeth*, and *Cymbeline*; the remaining fourteen complement – and complicate the textual status of – those plays that had previously been printed in quarto: *The Merry Wives of Windsor, Much Ado About Nothing, Love's Labours Lost,*

A Midsummer Night's Dream, *The Merchant of Venice*, *Richard II*, *1 Henry IV*, *2 Henry IV*, *Henry V*, *2 Henry VI*, *3 Henry VI*, *Richard III*, *Titus Andronicus*, *Hamlet**, *King Lear*, and *Othello*. (Additionally, four of the six undivided plays – *2 Henry VI*, *3 Henry VI*, *Troilus and Cressida*, and *Romeo and Juliet* – fall into this category.) The diverse provenance of the source texts for these plays gives the lie to Heminges and Condell's notorious dismissal of the quartos as 'stoln, and surreptitious copies, maimed, and deformed by the fraude and stealthes of iniurious imposters' (F1623, A3), since, as scholars have shown, in a number of cases these early editors of Shakespeare drew directly on previously printed versions they affected to discredit; it might also serve as a warning to those who seek to make coherent sense of the First Folio's structural diversity. In recent years, however, scholars have focused particularly on the wider (rather than 'merely' textual) implications of the Q-F dynamic where versions exist in both states. While editors are faced with theoretical and practical issues when confronted with multiple texts, critics have sought to explain why these different versions exist at all.

For Andrew Gurr, Shakespeare wrote longer plays (that would be incorporated into the First Folio) which the players cut down for performance (Gurr 1999). Conversely, challenging the long-established view that Shakespeare was not concerned with the printing of his plays, Lukas Erne argues that the shorter (Q) versions were designed for performance while the longer F-texts were prepared specifically for readers (Erne 2003). Richard Dutton returns the issue to the realm of performance. Rather than distinguishing only between Q/F texts he proposes that longer texts – for example, Q2 *Romeo and Juliet*, F *Henry V*, F *The Merry Wives of Windsor*, and Q2 and F *Hamlet* – represent performance at court, on the basis that longer performances were possible there. For James Hirsch, working in a long tradition of scholarship that has sought to resolve the puzzle of act-division in the 1623 compendium, these features are entirely divorced from performance: they are compositors' additions made in the printing-house, with no connection to either playwright or playhouse (Hirsh 2002); or, at an earlier stage of transmission, 'the classicizing gestures of a professional scribe', such as Ralph Crane (Turner 2006, 180).

But the Globe-Blackfriars conundrum remains. Reading longer texts as court productions does not help resolve issues of company repertory management. Gurr, Erne, and Dutton seek an explanation for these longer texts, each positing (to different ends) a particular scenario that makes sense of the Q-F relationship (or, for Dutton, Q-Q as well). Such an enquiry is beyond the scope of this Element on practical grounds, but we still lack a credible explanation for the non-division of all but a single quarto and the division of 80 per cent of the First Folio texts. In the light of the data analysis presented earlier, it would seem unlikely that the printing of act-divisions in the First Folio, fifteen years after the company began staging plays with intervals, was unconnected to the Blackfriars operation. Clues might lie in the treatment of act-breaks, and specifically the use of music. One characteristic worth exploring further is how Folio texts make use of the 2/3 interval – eleven plays suggesting some sort of pattern perhaps. Indeed, that we find cornets rather than trumpets indoors (Lindley 2009, 34–35) offers another text-based route to ascertaining provenance in the First Folio. There is no 'code', but (potentially) clues.

5.2.1 The Tempest

Identified as having been designed specifically for performance indoors (Wells 1979, Gurr 1989), *The Tempest* might offer a starting point for a wider analysis of the provenance of First Folio texts that feature act-divisions. Scholars have noted that at 4/5 Prospero and Ariel exit, and then re-enter, yet some critics believe that the play could as easily have been performed at the Globe as at the Blackfriars (Shakespeare, 1999), noting its apparent amphitheatre characteristics (Dustagheer 2017, 117, 120–1; Munro 2020, 128–31). Courtesy of the interval, they re-enter, Prospero '(*in his Magicke robes*)' (TLN1946) – a costume change the act-break facilitates; and, as Andrew Gurr points out, elsewhere in the play (1.2, 3.3, and 4.1), Shakespeare carefully calculates the time needed for Ariel to exit, change costume, and reappear (Gurr 1989, 94–95). David Lindley suggests that when Ferdinand says, 'I heare it now aboue me' (TLN550) he is referring to the musicians on the balcony, a feature of the Blackfriars theatre, rather than the Globe, in this, 'Shakespeare's most musical play' (Lindley 2009, 36, 37), and recent work has focused on the play's acoustic signature (e.g. Dustagheer 2017, 116–23), as far as this can be deduced from the 1623 text. These details point to indoor performance.

Like all indoor plays *The Tempest* was part of a musical *event*. Attending to the music (and acoustic effects) *within* the play tells only part of the story. As noted earlier, music bookended these plays, prefacing the opening scene and following the Epilogue. The play's 'amphitheatre-esque' opening scene would indeed have been striking indoors, and perhaps all the more so since it followed up to an hour of music of a presumably less discordant kind. Moreover, at each act-break non-diegetic(?) music would have added to and complicated the play's acoustic narrative in ways we cannot reconstruct; but in the light of critical attention to the significance of *The Tempest*'s music its indoor provenance invites us to speculate about the acoustic event of which the play is a (main, but not whole) part. For example, at each of the first three acts breaks the main plot gives way to the subplot (1/2, 3/4), or vice-versa (2/3), while at 4/5 of course the main plot continues through the LRE-interval: if (and, if so, how) the music was designed to fit this narrative structure, then any discussion of the *play*'s soundscape in isolation misses much of the acoustic experience that evidently was an important feature of its performance.

In another respect the play's likely provenance is invaluable for what it might tell us about the deeper structural implications that faced indoor playmakers, and how an understanding of the logistics of theatres such as Blackfriars provides insights into the making of plays there and elsewhere. In composing the play for Blackfriars Shakespeare had to calculate that the shipwreck scene, followed by the much longer expository sequence, would be within the maximum time that candles might realistically last until the first interval. Unlike *A Midsummer Night's Dream* and *Titus Andronicus*, this did not involve the makeshift insertion of act-breaks, but deliberate design. In respect of the First Folio *The Tempest* is the exception, but both within that collection and beyond, in the King's Men repertory in which it operated, it is surely a significant text for what it might tell us about indoor playmaking. While scholars continue to puzzle over both the length of some Shakespeare plays and, where they exist in more than one witness, Q/F variation, attention might turn to the issue of *act* length, and dramatic structure, at this indoor theatre over three decades but also in other indoor spaces.

5.3 Outdoor Intervals?

Unless, of course, the company anticipated what scholars today deduce was logically the next step. Amphitheatre intervals were an obvious solution to the issue of repertory management faced by the King's Men. Gary Taylor's proposal *might* find support in Richard Braithwait's *Whimʒies: or a New Cast of Characters* (1631), where the typical behaviour of a 'Ruffian' is presented by Clitus-Alexandrinus:

> To a play they will hazard to go, though with never a rag of money: where after the *second Act*, when the *Doore* is weakly guarded, they will make *forcible entrie*, a knock with a Cudgell is the worst; whereat though they grumble, they rest pacified upon their admittance. Forthwith by violent assault and assent, they aspire to the two-pennie roome; where being furnished with Tinder, Match, and a portion of decayed *Barmoodas*, they smoake it most terribly, applaude a prophane jest unmeasurably, and in the end grow distastefully rude to all the Companie. At the Conclusion of all, they single out their *dainty Doxes*, to cloze up a fruitlesse day with a sinnefull evening. (Braithwait 1631, 134–35; qtd. in Gurr 2004, 286; italics original)

It's a familiar story, the disreputable playhouse associated with vulgarity and vice. But two details are particularly significant: *when* the 'ruffians' enter the theatre, and *where* they 'aspire' to sit. If 'after the *second Act*' is accurate rather than impressionistic then they appear to have forced their way into a playhouse where act-breaks were observed – except that the 'two-pennie roome' or gallery was a feature of the *amphitheatre*, not the hall playhouse. Moreover, 'ruffians' lacking means are unlikely patrons of the Blackfriars or Phoenix, whose tariff began at between three and six pennies and went up to thirty (Gurr 2004, 31), and whose '*Doore*' would be closed rather than 'weakly guarded'. Braithwait does not identify the venue (common in such sketches), but the point of the satire is its general application. ('Forthwith' *may* indicate that they do not pass through the yard to access the galleries but go directly, as seems to have become the custom in the later amphitheatres such as the Globe and Fortune; see Gurr 2004, 17–19.) So, is this evidence? That the interval was adopted outdoors is not proven by this reference to people entering just before act 3 (a practice, incidentally, that would be regularised in the Restoration) but '*second Act*' is suggestive. How would these 'ruffians' *know* that two acts had passed? Outside an indoor theatre they would perhaps hear the music announcing the interval; perhaps it was the same at amphitheatres, if intervals were adopted there too, with music – and, perhaps, especially if sometimes it had been tolerated outdoors (Thomson 2010), stage-sitting came with it. Either Braithwait is calling up the established, 'classical' notion of drama that bears no relation to amphitheatre staging or registering an imported practice that Taylor deduces on other grounds.

5.4 Jacobean-Caroline Repertory Management

Further support *may* be found in several company trajectories, though, as with the King's Men, the precise arrangements remain murky. Over a short period of time three troupes *and/or* their plays moved between venue types, in both directions: indoor > outdoor > indoor; outdoor > indoor > outdoor. How this series of intersecting, cross-code movements worked is far from clear, but the practicalities involved pose questions regarding repertory management and staging practices that might contribute to our knowledge of these lesser-known companies.

The consequences of Christopher Beeston's decision to adapt a building in Drury Lane as an indoor theatre to which he could relocate his Red Bull company and their repertory are well known. A year later, in 1617, the Cockpit was wrecked on Shrove Tuesday by apprentices apparently angered by the move, since the more expensive playhouse was beyond their means. Beeston's company, Queen Anne's (formerly Worcester's) Men, had operated outdoors since their inception in 1603; however it was that they adapted their operation for the Cockpit, once it was unusable they had to return to the Red Bull, where they remained until the rebuilt, renamed Phoenix was ready the following year. That there seems to have been some repertory continuity in this sequence does not square easily with the traditional binary scholars have invested in, since it suggests that Beeston believed that what worked at the Red Bull would not be out of place at the Drury Lane theatre. Presumably company staples such as Heywood's plays were adjusted accordingly.

By way of illustration, *The Two Merry Milkmaids* presents an interesting puzzle. Printed in quarto in 1620, this Queen Anne's Men play was probably staged the previous year – but where? The question invites an answer in the plural. Leslie Thomson proposes that this play by 'J.C.' was originally written for the Cockpit but (also?) performed at the Red Bull (Thomson 1996, 200), the Prologue entreating

> All that are hither come,
> To expect no noyse of Guns, Trumpets, nor Drum,
> Nor sword and Targuet; but to heare Sence and Words,
> Fitting the matter that the Scene affords. (1–4)

In the absence of these typical amphitheatre features, it goes on: 'We hope, for your owne good, you in the Yard / Will lend your Eares, attentiuely to heare / Things that shall flow so smoothly to your eare' (10–12). This does indeed suggest a Cockpit > Red Bull trajectory. However, Q's address 'The Printer to the Reader' declares conversely that 'It was made more for the Eye, then the Eare' (8–9): how to explain this contradiction, pivoting on a sensory opposition, if it is such?

It may be significant that Q's paratext for the reader gestures (wryly?) to a situation that fits a dual-playhouse scenario: 'Every writer must gouerne his Penne according to the Capacitie of the Stage he writes too [sic], both in the Actor and the Auditor' (1–3). Innocuous enough, in the nature of printed prefatory material, but tantalising in this instance. The title-page claim that the play was staged at court is borne out by external records, which might be further supported by its being a very long play – some 3,600 lines (Thomson 1996, 188). Might this play fit a court-performance interpretation (though Dutton 2016 does not include it in his study), in which case Q may be closer to what was staged in a royal palace than at either of the London theatres? Whatever the provenance of the manuscript underpinning Q, the printed text itself does register the characteristics of indoor performance. Divided into acts, at two points the LRE restriction is evaded (2/3 and 3/4). Moreover, most interestingly an annotated (incomplete) copy of Q survives – but for what sort of performance(s)?

If the marked-up quarto Leslie Thomson examines does not date from either the 1662–63 revival (Thomson 1996, 202) or an unknown private performance during the Interregnum, it would seem that it registers the play's early staging history. This quarto features two (main) hands, each of which coincides with and diverges from the other: it is likely that 'the differences between their annotations reflect different productions, times, venues, and probably also acting companies' (Thomson 1996, 181). Interestingly, unlike the King's Men with *A Midsummer Night's Dream* and *Titus Andronicus*, bookkeepers 'A' and 'B' both cut chunks of dialogue; most significantly, while Q marks act-breaks, they are particularly alert to what is needed in the tiring-house during – as well as leading up to – the act-time. Apart from at the very end of *The Two Merry Milkmaids*, which concludes with a dance accompanied by music, Q signals 'musicke' at only one act-break, an sd at the beginning of act 3; if this is a new strain it followed interval music, but since 2/3 is a LRE-interval it may well be that the music was continuous, from the end of act 2, across the interval, and into the next act. Working from within the tiring-house (figuratively speaking), both A and B augment Q's act-breaks. A marks 1/2 'Longe' (cf. *Believe As You List* MS and Q *1 Fair Maid of the West*), leaving the other three act-markers untouched, while B adds 'Act' at 2/3, 3/4, and 4/5 (without altering A's 'Longe'). A and B judge Q's act-breaks to be insufficient: 'Act', for act-time, restores the interval that was significant in performance, not least for the bookkeeper, less so for the reader. This reminds us that printed quartos only sometimes (and usually accidentally) retain traces of behind-the-scenes preparation, and that 'act-breaks required special preparations' (Thomson 1996, 188). Thus the significance of additions such as at the beginning of act 2 – A inserts '[hob]oyes' and B 'Flourish' (Thomson 1996, 190) – is that these are tiring-house cues. Elsewhere this marked-up copy reveals preparatory notes, for a table, bed, but the emphasis given to the structuring of the performance through the interval is particularly striking.

Possibly Q reveals more than one staging trajectory, and that at an extra-textual level the annotated quarto registers distinctive adaptations for different theatrical scenarios (though in both cases with an interval structure). In their desire to match text to venue scholars are understandably invested in establishing a one-to-one correspondence. But as well as evidence (usually of a paratextual nature) that the printed text does *not* always reflect the play as staged (e.g. *1&2 Tamburlaine*, *The Duchess of Malfi*), we ought to consider more readily the possibility that a printed play sometimes registered a *composite* performance history. It may be, then, that Q represents neither '*the* play-text' nor (given the presence of bookkeepers A and B together) '*a* play-text' as such. Whether or not this is so, the Janus-faced paratextual apparatus suggests a flexibility in the company's operations that (predating this play) began with Beeston's outdoors > indoors initiative, continued with the 1617 reversal, and was maintained when the Cockpit was resurrected as the Phoenix in 1618.

Less well known is the toing and froing between Salisbury Court, and two long-established amphitheatres: the Fortune and Red Bull. Some of these arrangements may have been pre-planned: the men behind the new venture in 1629 were Richard Gunnell, who managed the Fortune, and the deputy Master of the Revels, William Blagrave; at any rate there is a discernible three-year pattern that may not have been mere happenstance. The reasons for these migrations are less significant than that they were (or were made) feasible, through repertory management. Thus, one or both of two scenarios apply: the conditions of playing at the two venue types were sufficiently complementary to facilitate ease of inter-theatre movement, and/or play design was simplified on a 'one size fits all' (both) basis. We can test these hypotheses against several of the admittedly small number of plays dateable to the various cycles in the sequence.

Although little information prior to their appearance at Salisbury Court survives, the King's Revels Men was an established company when Gunnell brought them to open his new theatre. They would be associated with Salisbury Court for two years (1629–1631), following which they went to the Fortune (1631–1634), before moving back to the indoor venue in 1634; the long plague closure of 1636–1637 brought their career to an end. Dates of composition and performance are rarely determinable with accuracy and the company's indoor/outdoor/indoor operations were all rather brief. Still, it is notable that three plays from the first of these tenures all exploit the interval for LRE purposes: *The Muses' Looking-Glass* (1/2, 2/3, 3/4, 4/5) and *Amyntas* (2/3) – both 1630 – and *Holland's Leaguer* (1/2, 3/4), the following year. Perhaps the company expected to remain at Gunnell's new theatre; at any rate these plays in the form they have come down to us could only be staged unchanged at the Fortune if intervals had been adopted there. A clue may lie in the fact that several plays corresponding to the Fortune years (1631–1634) – *Changes*, *The Sparagus Garden*, *The Lady Mother* – do *not* use the LRE-interval device; conversely, several plays dated to 1634 onwards, the year the company returned to Salisbury Court, do: *Messalina* (2/3) and *The Rebellion* (2/3).

These last two are particularly interesting. Richards's and Rawlin's plays *may* have been written for the Fortune – *if* intervals had been adopted there; more likely, they were composed for performance at Salisbury Court. If they both date from 1634 – *The Rebellion* is sometimes given a much earlier as well as a later date – we might tentatively conclude that the dramatists were exploiting stagecraft possibilities that were not available at the Fortune. This is not evidence in itself of distinct repertories, which would be inefficient and inflexible. Rather, it may well suggest that the company believed this switch to be its last; which, courtesy of the 1636–1637 plague, it was.

In the three years they spent at the Fortune the King's Revels Men were replaced at Salisbury Court by Prince Charles's Men; in 1634, when the King's Revels Men returned, it moved to the Red Bull, and at the general closure of the theatres in 1642 the company was to be found at the Fortune. This pattern, outdoor > indoors > outdoors, is the inverse of the career of the King's Revel's Men. But like that company, at least initially, they must have relied on their amphitheatre repertory and adapted these plays accordingly. One trace of this survives in the old amphitheatre play *Edmond Ironside*, mentioned previously, which exists in a marked-up MS with added act-breaks for revival by the company at Salisbury Court. In one instance, therefore, we have evidence of outdoor > indoor adaptation by Prince Charles's Men which was probably not an anomaly. Only two plays are associated with their tenure at Salisbury Court (*A Fine Companion* and *Tottenham Court* – the second of which is open to debate), and neither exploits the LRE-interval. However it approached working in an indoor playhouse, it would seem that its return to the Red Bull was eased by its established amphitheatre repertory, while its newer plays for Salisbury Court could be readily adapted. More than this, the slightness of the evidence makes it impossible to say with confidence.

Each of these cases poses several questions, none of which may be answered with any certainty. First, whether these arrangements were pre-planned or (more likely) contingent on circumstances and events. Second, how (in either scenario) these companies managed their repertories. It is surely unlikely that there was no cross-code movement between these amphitheatres and Salisbury Court (for which *Edmund Ironside* provides evidence), so the third question – or rather logical deduction – is that these companies, faced with the practical issues discussed previously, adapted plays accordingly. And yet the possibility that by the 1630s the interval convention had spread outdoors qualifies any (tentative) conclusions drawn. One further observation may be made, however. *If*, in the course of its summer operations, there was sufficient *natural* light at the Salisbury Court playhouse (about which we know frustratingly little) so that candles were not necessary (Graves 1999, 130), the question as to whether act-breaks featured at all arises. As with the question of outdoor intervals, it would seem likely that they did: that the feature was about much more than candle-mending.

Theatre historians have debated the significance of certain moments, such as the Privy Council's intervention in 1594, or the royal patronage of 1603, and few would dispute the importance of the King's Men's initiative in 1608. But access to the Blackfriars seems to have done much more than secure the company's long-term financial health. In part, it consolidated a long-standing aspect of professional playing – adaptability – that spread elsewhere. The driver of change in the long term was the candle – and the interval was the outcome.

6 Coda

Recovering the interval raises a whole host of questions, some of which have been identified in the preceding pages; others might open up further lines of enquiry. The focus of this Element, how play-texts register the act-time, so that its significance in performance and for repertory management might be better understood, invites further reflection on the presentation of this drama today, in the theatre and in the academy.

6.1 Performance

Typically, in modern productions we encounter this drama not with act-breaks, but with an *intermission* that often does not coincide with any of the original interval-points. Shakespeare's Globe, conceived as a collaborative, commercial-scholarly venture, positions itself as both public educator and academic partner; yet it is difficult to square this ethos with its perpetuation of an anachronistic, modern convention. Inserting one or more breaks in the action at the new Globe – as experimented with in its early years (Kiernan 1999, 121–2) – while SWP productions feature a single interval, points to a confusion of purpose. Perhaps the King's Men did eventually introduce intervals on the Bankside, but treating indoor plays as no different, structurally, from a National Theatre or RSC production undermines the SWP's claim to represent a Jacobean indoor theatre and its OPs.

The rationale behind Sam Wanamaker's project was precisely that it would depart from the practices of the modern theatre, rematching texts to their original conditions of performance – insofar as they could be replicated – as William Poel had attempted less ambitiously a century before. That remains its remit. Famously, when the new Globe opened, its 'groundlings' were encouraged to behave like modern sports fans. Space constraints may explain its decision not to follow the ASC project in Staunton, Virginia, in providing seating on the stage, but it is ironic that in its ostentatious pursuit of 'authenticity' – notably in the use of candlelight and its aesthetic effects, but also the function of music in early modern playmaking – the SWP has ignored one (or *four*) of the most distinctive OPs.

Perhaps, given the SWP's partial reliance on scholarly expertise, this failing is understandable. But it calls attention to a fundamental misapprehension more generally, that the interval is trans-historical. This confusion is apparent in Michael Billington's expression of irritation on the occasion when the SWP *did* use four act-breaks – unavoidably, since the play in question was *The Knight of the Burning Pestle* (Billington 2014); the *Guardian*'s theatre critic had previously considered how sometimes intervals sap a production of energy and momentum (Billington 2011). This would seem to be a view the Globe policymakers share. Despite its dismissal of other inconveniences – standing in the yard, inclement weather, poor sightlines in some parts of both spaces, uncomfortable seating – in this respect the Bankside enterprise has shown itself to be susceptible to modern sensibilities at the expense of its own raison d'être. Thus far, at least, the SWP has missed a wonderful opportunity to reinstate a feature that was of significance at every stage of an indoor play's trajectory – from conception to theatrical realization.

Unfortunately, for all that this indoor space is presented, like its sibling, as a 'replica' early modern theatre, in an important sense they are opposed. The SWP is recognizably the precursor of the modern, roofed theatre that marks a fundamental departure from the looking-back-to-the-Romans amphitheatre; its preoccupation with historical lighting technology paradoxically reinforces the view that this 'archetype' is in most respects – unlike its outdoor space – a proto-*modern* performance space, anticipating future theatre developments, rather than looking back to the Jacobean era it claims to evoke. While both theatres aim at a historical specificity *architecturally*, it seems that performance matters are left entirely to individual directors: like the Globe, the SWP tends to use the 'space in a way for which we have no historical warrant . . . [which] distorts how that space may have read and functioned for Jacobean performers and audiences' (Syme 2018, 143). In this context the interval is a casualty of disjointed thinking more broadly. And as Janette Dillon has observed, '[p]resent day performances have their own value, but as evidence they speak to us about today's performers and audiences, not about the nature of historical performances or printed texts' (Dillon 1994, 82). Given its aims and claims, the SWP should not be vulnerable to such a charge. That recent London productions of Ibsen and Chekhov have experimented with more than one interval, thus reinstituting the original performance structure (Lawson 2016), makes the SWP failure all the more glaring.

For SWP theatregoers, uneven artificial illumination, operated not by offstage computer (unlike its faux 'daylight' in the windowless auditorium, produced by electric light) but by visible, human agents (usually outwith the play-world fiction but always within the performance event), ought surely to be part of the defamiliarization ethos ostensibly central to the Shakespeare's Globe concept. Inter alia, restoring intervals as the aural-visual theatre-units they were would help underpin the project's overall aim, which is to challenge a modern audience's assumptions and expectations through exposure to *historical*, distinctly *un*modern practices. Currently, this is not the case, but what better way to call attention to the (sparkling) jewel(s) in SWP's crown, much lauded in SWP-related scholarship (White 2014; Dustagheer 2017, 123–38; Tosh 2018, 91–118), than to reinstitute the device that made the candlelit indoor theatre possible?

6.2 Print

In the academy, too, we have lost sight of the interval. Ironically, the ubiquitous five-act structure in modern editions serves less to draw attention to the act-time than obscure it, privileging a misunderstood literary form over actual early modern practice. As much as editors today recognize the importance of conveying a play's performance history, this aim is compromised by the studied literariness of the text's layout. A key issue, then, is how might modern editions accurately represent, *and* distinguish between, indoor and outdoor practices? At present, for the most part (excepting those few plays editors divide into scenes alone or an even smaller number presented undivided) modern editions look very much the same. Thus both traditions are misrepresented: we read into divided plays a structure that the amphitheatre ignored, and fail to appreciate what act-breaks actually signified in the hall playhouse.

Something of this disconnect is illustrated in a recent edition of one of the few indoor plays to have been printed undivided. Here editors face a dilemma. Thomas Middleton's *The Phoenix* was staged by the Children of Paul's in 1603, at court in early 1604, and printed by Edward Allde for Arthur Johnson in 1607 (Taylor and Lavagnino 2007a, 91; 2007b, 529). An editor is faced with the choice of privileging Q – the copy-text, after all – over theatre provenance, *or* finding four places where breaks in the action might be inserted, mapping onto Q a five-act structure. Unlike previous editors – who, no doubt, were guided by classical 'tradition' – the Oxford Middleton editors follow Q, which they divide into scenes. A reference to *'the music'* (10.0sd) leads them to conclude that while Middleton was writing for indoor conditions, Q 'was not set from a theatrical manuscript or a literary transcript, either of which would have been likely to indicate [act] divisions'; to introduce such a structure would be 'arbitrary' (Taylor and Lavagnino 2007b, 529).

In this scenario, what should editors do? There is no clear-cut answer. Q misrepresents the play as staged; and, Lawrence Danson and Ivo Kamps argue, it is significantly removed from the author's conception (or indeed the company's). To import act-divisions would only be 'arbitrary', however, if it were a purely *literary*/editorial measure, which the introduction of *scene* divisions (for an *indoor* play) unquestionably is. The music signal – *'Exeunt. / Toward the close of the musick, the Iustices three men prepare for a robberie'* (Q1607, F3) – is strong evidence for a break in performance at this point, but more significantly is the re-entry here, *'Enter Iustice Falso, vntrust'* (F3v): a clear instance of the LRE-interval in operation. Thus, Q *does* register provenance, partially. Somehow, it would seem, in the MS > print process, the structure required for this text to work indoors has been lost. A modern editorial calculation backwards and forwards from this point would produce *a* five-act structure, as Paul's required, even if this approach would permit several permutations, rather than achieve a 'restoration' as such. Although choices would have to be made, a full explanation of the process (and the alternative possibilities) would go some way towards aligning the edition with indoor practices. But even so, the outcome would still be a conventional five-act play, not in itself, *today*, a marker of indoor practice – unless something were to be envisaged on a more ambitious scale.

Several solutions suggest themselves. The *Norton Shakespeare* prints parallel Q-/F-based *King Lear*s (as well as a composite text), though does not follow suit with *Hamlet*, *Othello*, and so on; one could see how a similar approach might work with Shakespeare Q/F versions, taking each on its merits, *if* a convincing case could be made for outdoor/indoor provenance respectively. (But that, most certainly, is a question for another day.)

The difficulty here is that Shakespeare editing is a matter of tradition rather than innovation, ease of referencing privileged over all else. The Arden 3 *Titus Andronicus* accommodates both Qq's (*implied*) scene breaks *and* where F diverges, as in the opening sequence with the imposition of 1/2, and the other three act-breaks. Here is a very basic model of an overlaid editorial apparatus, offering the reader an impression of outdoor/indoor practice simultaneously – which would be a natural fit for a digital format. Electronic platforms might be a better host for presenting layers of information operating on distinct planes of reference. In place of the printed 'critical *edition*', a 'critical *archive*' (Massai 2004, 103; italics original) might therefore register a play's stage history – its trajectory between theatre types – which print fixes at/as a single venue-type. However, none of these solutions addresses the core issue.

The fundamental problem goes much deeper. Clearly one reason for our neglect of the interval is that it has left so few traces. This is not solely a question of the likely omission of 'intertexts', such as has been documented elsewhere (Stern 2009, 2018) and may apply to act-time business. If the 'standard' activity – music with a dancing boy – was commonly the responsibility of the company, it is unsurprising that it was mostly unrecorded; regardless that this aural-visual effect was part of the performance, perhaps the various agents involved in the dissemination of drama as it moved from playhouse to printing-house did not regard it as a key part of the play – or, indeed, representable in print. Uniformity may have been a factor, most plays *not* featuring specific business in the act-time. But it presents a conundrum, nevertheless, because even where there *is* scripted business the established mise-en-page is unable to accommodate it. The issue is one of form, rather than content. Whatever its effect in the theatre, and on playmaking culture, Marston's innovative act-time business or Beaumont's and Jonson's scripted stage-sitting did not lead to innovation in the layout of printed drama. *The Knight of the Burning Pestle* even omits the horizontal dividing line we find separating acts in *The Staple of News* and *The Magnetic Lady*, and elsewhere. In several Marston plays the scripting of the act-time is placed at the *beginning* of the act it precedes. Nowhere, anywhere, is there an attempt to place act-time business in such a way that it is represented as being *between* the acts.

To take one example, presumably the italicized, parenthesized sd in *The Changeling* conveyed sufficient information for the Interregnum reader:

> *Alon.* Thanks kind *Deflores.*
> *Def.* He's safely thrust upon me beyond hopes   *Exeunt:*

ACTUS TERTIUS.

Enter Alonʒo and Deflores.
(*In the Act time Deflores hides a naked Rapier.*)

(Q1653, D3v)

'Parenthesis simultaneously subordinated *and* drew attention to the words inside the brackets' (Bourne 2020b, 202; italics original) – a formulation that fits nicely De Flores's use of the act-time (Hutchings 2011, 102–9). But the reader of Q1653 understands this sequence achronologically. Only *after* the new act is signalled, and the characters enter, is the parenthesized interval business revealed, which requires a rereading of the sequence – if not immediately, subsequently, for there is no sd to indicate that De Flores retrieves the rapier he has hidden before disarming his victim at the beginning of act 3 and then killing him. Here and elsewhere, there is no *place* for this business as such; the act-time is *dis*placed, which presents editors with a problem (Hutchings 2011, 102). In modern eyes it might be argued that this 'delayed presentation' created a *frisson* – an equivalent, for the 17th-century reader, of the uncanny in the theatre; but the expedient, if it was, of using parenthesis was one solution to a problem caused by the lack of a specific textual apparatus that could (adequately) represent the act-time in print.

Curiously, for all his classicism, the act-divisions in Jonson's *Workes* (1616) are strikingly unobtrusive, marked (as are scenes) but lacking the horizontal dividing line found elsewhere. As Paul Menzer points out,

> print privileges the poetic line while ignoring the graphic, utile one. Print un-scores the text while unwittingly emphasizing the importance of verse as a formal performative feature, advancing poetry over performance. (Menzer 2013, 121)

This observation does more than fit the Jonson who is considered to privilege the 'poem' over the 'play', and – judging by his satirical portraits of stage-sitters in *The Staple of News* and *The Magnetic Lady* – clearly the interval was an anathema to a writer who feared loss of authority in the theatre (which, however obliquely, the horizontal line gestures towards). But interestingly, those plays in the 1616 collection reprinted in the posthumous *Workes* (1641–1642) *do* feature such horizontal lines demarcating act-breaks, 'restored' by agents unknown. And yet in other respects he *was* inventive with the *mise-en-page*. Like several dramatists, Jonson on occasion, 'in collaboration with compositors, printers, and publishers, attempted to recapture in print the principle of supplementary signification that lies at the heart of theatrical representation' by using marginal space for additional sd material, thus 'construct[ing] an alternative mode of theatricality' on the page (Syme 2008, 149, 144). To convey simultaneity in dialogue and action such use of the margin – otherwise unused white space, which therefore did not increase the amount of paper required – was ideal, since this facilitated left-to-right reading of distinct planes of theatrical signification together; more generally, the *mise-en-page* '[taught] readers how to navigate and encounter the texts in front of them as *plays*' (Bourne 2020b, 194; italics original). Unlike the representation of the act-time at 2/3 in *The Changeling*, in the absence of a generic apparatus the margin could also be used in this way. In *The Two Noble Kinsmen* (Q1634), at 2/3 the act-time business is placed in the right-hand margin: 'Cornets in / sundry places. / Noise and / hallowing as / people a May- / ing'. is aligned roughly opposite the last line of act 2 and the first of act 3, straddling 'Actus Tertius'. sandwiched between two horizontal lines (F2r). In these Middleton and Rowley and Shakespeare and Fletcher examples we may read the respective *mises-en-page* as innovative, but they also point to a problem: what was (predominantly, but not exclusively) tiring-house activity was not translated into a play-text component in the printing-house.

We might conclude that for early moderns their familiarity with theatre practices enabled them to interpret what (diverse) signalling there was, at least once printed drama had established its own conventions. But in the 16th century at least, guidance was required. Claire Bourne has shown how, early on, steps were taken to shape these texts for the reader (Bourne 2020a, 32–76). The pilcrow (¶), as well as other glyphs, demarcated features in the printed play (speeches, character, action) to provide a 'visual scaffolding' (Bourne 2020a, 58); in *Gorboduc*, for example, aligning ¶ with each of the dumb show headings structures the reader's experience of the play in print, 'partition[ing] the play into five parts' (Bourne 2020a, 64). Her conclusion that these symbols were eventually rendered obsolete as readers became accustomed to reading plays, such signals being superseded by blank space – 'typographical absence instead of presence' (Bourne 2020a, 70) – may partly explain why an apparatus for the interval did not emerge, the graphic line(s) aside. With respect to the structure of performance, given educated readers' familiarity with the five-act model and its adoption by the indoor theatres, it would seem that little further help was regarded as necessary, let alone desirable. That glyphs fall out of use late in the Elizabethan period (Bourne 2020a, 73–5), just when the market for printed drama was growing, suggests that the eventual standardization of printed act-breaks in the 17th century (Taylor 1993, 4) was sufficient for the reader to intuit the interval – especially *if* the act-time became the norm across the theatre landscape.

But *our* problem today is of a different order. Act-division markers ≠ the act-time. Undeniably, modern readers need guidance, as, in other respects, their forbears did. A new apparatus that accommodates the act-time business would have to distinguish between indoor and outdoor practices. The question is, how to address this issue, given that our misleading, 'editorial-composite' texts are firmly established in the academy?

The straitjacketing of editors has a long history. Samuel Johnson regarded the First Folio's 1/2 division in *Titus Andronicus* as erroneous, but retained it nevertheless (Bate 1995, 158n), and so have his successors. So, it may be 'time for editors to abandon the 18th-century neoclassical conventions of act divisions' (Bourus 2018, 180) – which would be appropriate for amphitheatre plays; but what of hall plays (and, indeed, those of dual-code provenance)? Regularization of format is part of a wider issue: 'modern alterations destroy a page design that achieves a theatrical effect in print' (Syme 2008, 152). Recognizing that early modern printing agents did not resolve what (to them) was not a problem but to us should be, it may be that recent commentary on editorial practices and possible alternative models (e.g. Kidnie 2004) might inform re-evaluation of the situation presented here.

Ironically, given the centuries of controversy over the significance of its act-divisions – a history of intractability such that no phrase is more apposite than 'there is no end in sight' – it is perhaps to the First Folio that we might (re)turn to address the issue. Whatever 'story' the act-divisions in the 1623 texts have to tell, the *mise-en-page* of the compendium offers an adaptive model. Throughout its divided plays, act designation within two horizontal lines, producing a boxed-off white space, offers a means of signalling indoor practice. All thirty divided plays mark act-breaks in this way; the Beamont and Fletcher 1647 Folio follows suit. These boxes have markedly less work to do than the single horizontal line in Jonson's *Workes* (1640–1641), and as a hybrid example of 'typographical absence' (Bourne 2020a, 70), they would offer a surrogate space for the act-time for today's users. Thus, 1/2 *Titus Andronicus* (F1623) –

Satur Be it so *Titus*, and Gramercy to.   *Exeunt*

Actus Secunda.

Flourish   *Enter Aaron alone.*

– might be adapted for a modern edition by moving '*Actus Secunda*' to the space below the second graphic line and above Aaron's entrance, thus repurposing the box as the space for the act-time (even if such activity, as in most cases, consisted solely of the formulaic music + dancing boy routine). Since 'readers construct meaning, not just by *reading* a page but by *looking at* a page' (Kidnie 2004, 169; italics original), an enhanced feature such as this might help restore the status of the interval and, conversely, allow readers to discriminate between indoor and outdoor practices, thus enhancing awareness of these overlapping though distinct performance traditions.

The problem identified here lies in the disjunction between an established editorial apparatus and the diverse conditions of early modern playmaking. Since it would be wholly unrealistic to challenge the referencing system on which the scholarly community continues to rely, the most reasonable solution (*pace* Bourus 2018, 180) would be to repurpose the act-division tradition as representing – where a convincing argument might be made – an *indoor* iteration of that play; at the same time, editions would steer readers towards an understanding that, *outdoors*, the five-act structure of modern editions does not represent performance at all – at least, *perhaps*, not until some point prior to 1642. Ironically, then, just as early modern playmakers adapted a misunderstood dramatic structure to solve a technological problem, today we might recognize that the apparatus scholars adopted and maintain for referencing purposes that have little to do with the 'default' amphitheatre OPs might indeed yet tell us a good deal about another performance practice, as the following LRE data suggests.

Appendix
The King's Men Repertory: Plays Acquired, 1609–1642

The strongest evidence for gauging how the interval influenced playmaking is LRE data, and here the King's Men's Globe-Blackfriars years provide much food for thought. With Bentley's dual-repertory theory currently out of favour, scholars suppose a vaguely fluid interchange between playhouses (and, indeed, other venues, such as royal palaces), of both pre- and post-1609 plays. It is a nice question whether the opening of the Blackfriars alone, the enforced (temporary) closure of the Globe in 1613–1614, or a combination of these and perhaps other factors were decisive in shaping the company's long-term repertory management. A long visitation of the plague from July 1608 to December 1609 prevented the company from playing at the Blackfriars until (probably) early 1610; Leeds Barroll is sceptical of the possibility that in order to practice for the court at this time the King's Men may have used the Blackfriars for rehearsal purposes (Barroll 2005, 159), but Blackfriars conditions would have been suitable, and if they did the actors would have had an opportunity to explore repertory management possibilities from the outset. Or, if a 'music room' was installed at the Globe sometime after 1609 (Ichikawa 2012, 68–69; qtd. in Fotheringham 2021, 24), it may be, given a *possible* association between this feature and the act-time, that this underpinned the introduction of intervals outdoors. But until firm evidence emerges to confirm that the Globe adopted intervals (and, if so, when), the growing consensus in favour of a cross-code, interchangeable repertory (e.g. Knutson 2006; Dustagheer 2017; Munro 2020) is open to challenge.

The following table lists 124 surviving plays (omitting 32 lost plays from the period and all pre-1609 plays, but including 11 acquired from other companies), with LRE status and title-page provenance (where indicated). The authority of title-page attributions is less secure than theatre historians would wish; however, the LRE-provenance correlation in the King's Men's repertory is suggestive. Where the title pages of plays that exploit the interval for LRE purposes state that they were staged at the Globe only (a mere eight in total), their reliability is open to question; conversely, where title pages allocate provenance to both playhouses (totalling seven), it might be suspected that Gary Taylor's conjecture about outdoor intervals is borne out. Beaumont and Fletcher's *Philaster* (1609) is a case in point. Q1 (1620) allocates it to the Globe, despite its use of the interval at 2/3 and 4/5; but Q2 (1622) and Q3 (1628) title pages (and several other subsequent printings) give it to both theatres. The King's Men may have been influenced by their predecessors at the Blackfriars. Of the plays known to have been staged there (1600–8), 13 of 21 feature the LRE-interval. (A further play in this group, *The Knight of the Burning Pestle*, uses the act-time in a different way of course.) For the years 1609–42 we find a similar proportion. Massinger's *The Emperor of the East* (1631) is particularly notable, since exceptionally it uses all four of its intervals in this way; the title page (Q1632) gives it to both playhouses. Of the 124 extant plays, in 71 (57 per cent) the LRE is accommodated through the use of act-breaks, and of the plays where title pages proclaim provenance 57 (89 per cent) are designated Blackfriars-only productions.

Taking the title-page information on its own, the preponderance of Blackfriars-only attributions in the Caroline era might suggest that the company and/or publishers sought to capitalize on the social cachet playmaking now enjoyed, which an indoor (rather than outdoor) theatre conveyed, particularly when court favour could be advertised as well. In print, then, the Globe's relative invisibility may be more apparent than real. But the LRE data tells a story of the interval that either confirms these ascriptions or supports Taylor's interpretation of the printing of act-divisions. Whether the company adopted intervals across the board from as early as 1609 or not long afterwards is the big question. What is incontrovertible is that indoor practices shaped – one might say defined – the King's Men's repertory over this thirty-year period

Date	Play	Dramatist(s)	Pub.	LRE	Title page / (Other)
[c?1594-1605]	Alphonsus, Emperor Of Germany Rev.?]	Peele? Chapman?	1654	–	Blackfriars*
[c.1603-1604]	Bussy D'Ambois	Chapman	1607	3/4, 4/5	–(Children of Paul's)]*
[c.1606	The Woman Hater	Beaumont	1607	–	–(Children of Paul's)]
[1608?	The Faithful Shepherdess	Fletcher	1609	–	1634: Blackfriars (Children of the Blackfriars)]*
[1608-1610]	The Coxcomb	Beaumont & Fletcher	1647c	–	–(Children of the Queen's Revels)]*
1609	Philaster	Beaumont & Fletcher	1620	2/3, 3/4, 4/5	Globe (1620); 1622, 1628: Globe & Blackfriars*
1609	Cymbeline	Shakespeare	1623c	–	–
[1609	Mucedorus	Anon.	1610 (Q3)	–	Globe (Company?)]*
[1609-1610]	Epicene	Jonson	1616c	2/3, 3/4	–(Children of the Queen's Revels)]*

(*cont.*)

Date	Play	Dramatist(s)	Pub.	LRE	Title page / (Other)
[1609–1612?]	*The Woman's Prize*	Fletcher	1647c	1/2, 3/4, 4/5	– (Company?)]*
[c.1610]	*The Scornful Lady*	Beaumont & Fletcher	1616	–	Blackfriars (Children of the Queen's Revels)]*
1610	*Valentinian*	Beaumont & Fletcher	1647c	1/2, 4/5	–
1610	*Bonduca*	Beaumont & Fletcher	1647c	3/4	–
1610	*The Alchemist*	Jonson	1612	3/4	– (1616c, King's Men)*
1610	*The Winter's Tale*	Shakespeare	1623c	–	–*
1610	*Catiline*	Jonson	1611	–	– (1616c, King's Men)
c.1610–1616	*Monsieur Thomas*	Fletcher	1639	1/2	Blackfriars

Date	Play	Dramatist(s)	Pub.	LRE	Title page / (Other)
1611	A King and No King	Beaumont & Fletcher	1619	–	Globe*
1611	The Tempest	Shakespeare	1623c	4/5	–*
1611	The Lady's Tragedy ['The Second Maiden's Tragedy']	Middleton	(MS)	–	–
c.1611	The Maid's Tragedy	Beaumont & Fletcher	1619	–	Blackfriars*
1612	The Captain	Beaumont & Fletcher	1647c	–	–*
1612	Henry VIII	Shakespeare & Fletcher	1623c	–	–
[1612-1613]	Cupid's Revenge	Beaumont & Fletcher	1615	–	– (Children of the Queen's Revels)]*
c.1612-1615?	Love's Cure	Beaumont & Fletcher (rev. Massinger, c.1625?)	1647c	4/5	–
[1613	The Honest Man's Fortune	Fletcher	1647c	4/5	– (Lady Elizabeth's Men)]
1613	The Duchess of Malfi	Webster	1623	3/4	Blackfriars & Globe*
1613	The Two Noble Kinsmen	Shakespeare & Fletcher	1634	–	Blackfriars

(*cont.*)

Date	Play	Dramatist(s)	Pub.	LRE	Title page / (Other)
1614	*More Dissemblers Besides Women*	Middleton	1657c	–	–*
c.1614–1615	*The Witch*	Middleton	MS	4/5	Blackfriars
1615	*Love's Pilgrimage*	Beaumont & Fletcher	1647c	–	–*
1615	*Thierry and Theodoret*	Fletcher & Massinger	1621	3/4	Blackfriars
1615	*The Laws of Candy*	Ford	1647c	2/3, 4/5	–
1615	*The Beggar's Bush*	Fletcher	1647c	1/2*, 3/4, 4/5	–*
1616	*The Devil is an Ass*	Jonson	1631	1/2, 3/4	–
1616	*The Queen of Corinth*	Fletcher	1647c	1/2, 4/5	–
1616	*The Widow*	Middleton	1652	–	Blackfriars
1616	*The Loyal Subject*	Fletcher	1647c	1/2, 4/5	–*
1616	*The Knight of Malta*	Fletcher, Field, Massinger	1647c	2/3	–
1616	*The Fatal Dowry*	Field & Massinger	1632	1/2, 4/5	Blackfriars*

				1/2, 2/3, 3/4	Blackfriars
c.1616–1620	Hengist, King of Kent	Middleton	1661		
1617	The Chances	Fletcher	1647c	3/4, 4/5	—*
1617	The Mad Lover	Fletcher	1647c	—	—*
1617	The Bloody Brother	Fletcher & Massinger	1639	—	—(Globe)*
1618	The Humourous Lieutenant	Fletcher	1647c	—	—
1618	The Little French Lawyer	Fletcher & Massinger	1647c	4/5	—
1618	The Duke of Milan	Massinger	1623	3/4	Blackfriars
1619	Sir John van Olden Barnavelt	Fletcher & Massinger	MS	—	—
1619	Women Pleased	Fletcher	1647c	—	—
1619	The Custom of the Country	Fletcher & Massinger	1647c	4/5	—*
1619	The Double Marriage	Fletcher & Massinger	1647c	—	—
1619	The False One	Fletcher & Massinger	1647c	3/4	—
1619	The Island Princess	Fletcher	1647c	2/3	—*

Date	Play	Dramatist(s)	Pub.	LRE	Title page / (Other)
c.1621	*Anything for a Quiet Life*	Middleton & Webster	1662	–	Blackfriars
1621	*The Pilgrim*	Fletcher	1647c	1/2, 2/3	–*
1621	*The Wild Goose Chase*	Fletcher	1652	4/5	Blackfriars*
?1622	*The Nice Valour*	Middleton (&?)	1647c	1/2	–
1622	*The Prophetess*	Fletcher & Massinger	1647c	1/2	–
1622	*The Sea Voyage*	Fletcher & Massinger	1647c	–	– (Globe)
1622	*The Spanish Curate*	Fletcher & Massinger	1647c	–	– (Blackfriars)*
1622	*Osmond the Great Turk*	Carlell	1657c	2/3	–
1623	*The Lovers' Progress*	Fletcher (rev. Massinger?)	1647c	2/3	–*
1623	*The Maid in the Mill*	Fletcher & Rowley	1647c	–	–*
1624	*Rule a Wife and Have a Wife*	Fletcher	1640	2/3, 4/5	–*
1624	*A Wife for a Month*	Fletcher	1647c	–	–*

1624	The Unnatural Combat	Massinger	1639	2/3	Globe
1624	A Game at Chess	Middleton	1625	–	Globe
1625	The Elder Brother	Fletcher & Massinger	1637	3/4	Blackfriars*
c.1626?	The Noble Gentleman	Beaumont & Fletcher	1647c	4/5	– (Blackfriars)
1626	The Fair Maid of the Inn	Fletcher (and other[s])	1647c	–	– (Blackfriars)
1626	The Staple of News	Jonson	1631c	N/A	–*
1626	The Roman Actor	Massinger	1629	1/2, 3/4	Blackfriars
1627	The Cruel Brother	Davenant	1630	4/5	Blackfriars
1628	The Lover's Melancholy	Ford	1629	–	Blackfriars & Globe
1628	The Deserving Favourite	Carlell	1629	1/2, 2/3, 3/4	Blackfriars*
1628	The Soddered Citizen	Clavell	MS	–	–
1629	The Northern Lass	Brome	1632	1/2, 2/3	Globe & Blackfriars*
1629	The Just Italian	Davenant	1630	–	Blackfriars
1629	The New Inn	Jonson	1631	4/5	–*
1629	The Picture	Massinger	1630	–	Globe & Blackfriars
1629	The Inconstant Lady	Wilson	MS	–	Blackfriars*

Date	Play	Dramatist(s)	Pub.	LRE	Title page / (Other)
1630	The Broken Heart	Ford	1633	–	Blackfriars
1631	The Queen's Exchange	Brome	1657	–	Blackfriars
1631	Believe As You List	Massinger	MS	–	–
1631	The Emperor of the East	Massinger	1632	1/2, 2/3, 3/4, 4/5	Blackfriars & Globe
1631	The Swisser	Wilson	MS	–	Blackfriars
1631	The Novella	Brome	1653	2/3	Blackfriars
1632	The Magnetic Lady	Jonson	1641c	N/A	–
1632	The City Madam	Massinger	1658	4/5	Blackfriars
1633	The Guardian	Massinger	1655	–	Blackfriars*
1633	Love and Honour	Davenant	1649	1/2, 2/3	Blackfriars*

1634	The Late Lancashire Witches	Heywood & Brome	1634	—	Globe
1634	The Courage of Love	Davenant	1649	1/2, 2/3	Blackfriars
1634	The Wits	Davenant	1636	4/5	Blackfriars*
1634	Albertus Wallenstein	Glapthorne	1639–1640	—	Globe
1634	A Very Woman	Massinger	1655	—	Blackfriars
1634	A Challenge for Beauty	Heywood	1636	4/5	Blackfriars & Globe
1635	News from Plymouth	Davenant	1673c	1/2	– (Blackfriars)
1635	The Platonic Lovers	Davenant	1636	1/2, 2/3, 4/5	Blackfriars
1635	The Conspiracy	Killigrew	1638	—	Blackfriars
1635	1 Arviragus and Philicia	Carlell	1639	3/4	Blackfriars*
1635	2 Arviragus and Philicia	Carlell	1639	—	Blackfriars*
1636	The Royal Slave	Cartwright	1639	3/4	*
1637	The Bashful Lover	Massinger	1655	1/2	Blackfriars
1637	The Lost Lady	Berkeley	1638	1/2, 2/3, 4/5	Blackfriars*
1637	The City Match	Mayne	1639	4/5	Blackfriars*

(cont.)

Date	Play	Dramatist(s)	Pub.	LRE	Title page / (Other)
1637	*Aglaura*	Suckling	1638	4/5	– (1646: Blackfriars)*
1637	*The Goblins*	Suckling	1646	1/2, 4/5	Blackfriars
1637	*1 The Passionate Lovers*	Carlell	1655	–	Blackfriars*
1637	*2 The Passionate Lovers*	Carlell	1655	1/2, 2/3	Blackfriars*
1638	*The Doubtful Heir*	Shirley	1652	2/3	Blackfriars
1638	*The Fair Favourite*	Davenant	1673c	1/2	–*
1638	*The Unfortunate Lovers*	Davenant	1643	1/2, 4/5	Blackfriars*
1639	*The Distresses*	Davenant	1673c	2/3	–
1639	*Brennoralt*	Suckling	1642	3/4, 4/5	– (1646: Blackfriars)
1639	*The Variety*	Cavendish	1649	1/2	Blackfriars
1640	*The Imposture*	Shirley	1652	1/2	Blackfriars
1640	*Queen of Aragon*	Habington	1640	–	Blackfriars*

1641?	The Country Captain	Cavendish	1649	–	Blackfriars
1641	The Sophy	Denham	1642	1/2, 2/3, 4/5	Blackfriars
1641	The Brothers	Shirley	1652	–	Blackfriars
1641	The Cardinal	Shirley	1652	3/4	Blackfriars
1642	The Sisters	Shirley	1652	3/4, 4/5	Blackfriars
1642	The Court Secret †	Shirley	1652	4/5	Blackfriars

Sources: Greg 1939–59; Harbage 1964; Gurr 1996, 2004; Astington 1999; Taylor and Lavagnino 2007b; Dustagheer 2014, 2017; Munro 2020. Square brackets indicate old plays acquired by the King's Men; c = collection (hence usually the title page does not indicate provenance); known court performance by the company is signalled thus *; ? registers uncertainty over dating, authorship, or company affiliation.

† 'Never Acted, / But prepared for the Scene at / Black-Friers', reads the title page, suggesting that the closure of the playhouses in late summer 1642 prevented its staging.

References

Astington, John. (1999). *English Court Theatre, 1558–1642*, Cambridge: Cambridge University Press.

Austern, Linda Phyliss. (1985–1986). Sweet Meats with Sour Sauce: The Genesis of Musical Irony in English Drama after 1600. *The Journal of Musicology* 4:4, 472–90.

Baldwin, T. W. (1947). *Shakspere's Five-Act Structure: Shakspere's Early Plays on the Background of Renaissance Theories of Five-Act Structure from 1470*, Urbana: University of Illinois Press.

Baldwin, T. W. (1965). *On Act and Scene Division in the Shakspere First Folio*, Carbondale and Edwardsville: Southern Illinois University Press.

Barroll, Leeds. (2005). Shakespeare and the Second Blackfriars Theater. *Shakespeare Studies* 33, 156–70.

Beaumont, Francis. (1984). *The Knight of the Burning Pestle*, ed., Sheldon P. Zitner. Manchester: Manchester University Press.

Beaumont, Francis. (2012). *The Honest Man's Fortune*, ed., Grace Ioppolo. Manchester: Manchester University Press.

Bentley, G. E. (1941–1968). *The Jacobean and Caroline Stage*. 7 Vols., Oxford: Clarendon Press.

Bentley, G. E. (1948). Shakespeare and the Blackfriars Theatre. *Shakespeare Survey* 1, 38–50.

Billington, Michael. (2011). Theatre Intervals: Is It Curtains? *The Guardian*, 1 March. www.theguardian.com/stage/theatreblog/2011/mar/01/theatre-intervals.

Billington, Michael. (2014). A Spirited Romp by Candlelight. *The Guardian*, 27 February. www.theguardian.com/stage/2014/feb/27/the-knight-burning-pestle-adele-thomas-review.

Blayney, Peter W. M. (1996). Ed. and Intro. *The First Folio of Shakespeare: Based on Folios in the Folger Shakespeare Library Collection Prepared by Charlton Hinman*, New York: W. W. Norton.

Bly, Mary. (2000). *Queer Virgins and Virgin Queans on the Early Modern Stage*, Oxford: Oxford University Press.

Bourne, Claire M. L. (2020a). *Typographies of Performance in Early Modern England*, Oxford: Oxford University Press.

Bourne, Claire M. L. (2020b). Typography *after* Performance. In Tiffany Stern, ed., *Rethinking Theatrical Documents in Shakespeare's England*, London: Bloomsbury, 193–215.

Bourus, Terri. (2018). Editing and Directing: *Mise en scene, mis en page*. In Sarah Dustagheer and Gillian Woods, eds., *Stage Directions and Shakespearean Theatre*, London: Bloomsbury, 163–87.

Bradley, David. (1992). *From Text to Performance in the Elizabethan Theatre: Preparing the Play for the Stage*, Cambridge: Cambridge University Press.

Braithwait, Richard. (1631). *Whimzies: or a New Cast of Characters*. London

Carson, Neil. (1988). *A Companion to Henslowe's Diary*, Cambridge: Cambridge University Press.

Chambers, E. K. (1923). *The Elizabethan Stage*. 4 Vols., Oxford: Clarendon Press.

Cohen, Ralph Alan. (2009). The Most Convenient Place: The Second Blackfriars Theater and Its Appeal. In Richard Dutton, ed., *The Oxford Handbook of Early Modern Theatre*, Oxford: Oxford University Press, 209–24.

Cotgrave, Randle. (1611). *A Dictionary of the French and English [T]ongues*, London.

Dekker, Thomas. (1606). *The Seven Deadly Sinnes of London*, London.

Dekker, Thomas. (1609). *The Guls Horne-Book*, London

Dessen, Alan C. and Leslie Thomson. (1999). *A Dictionary of Stage Directions in English Drama, 1580–1642*, Cambridge: Cambridge University Press.

Dillon, Janett. (1994). Is There a Performance in This Text? *Shakespeare Quarterly* 45, 74–86.

Dustagheer, Sarah. (2014). Appendix: List of Plays Performed at Indoor Playhouses, 1575–1642. In Andrew Gurr and Farah Karim-Cooper, eds., *Moving Shakespeare Indoors: Performance and Repertoire in the Jacobean Playhouse*, Cambridge: Cambridge University Press, 252–9.

Dustagheer, Sarah. (2017). *Shakespeare's Two Playhouses: Repertory and Theatre Space at the Globe and the Blackfriars, 1599–1613*, Cambridge: Cambridge University Press.

Dutton, Richard. (2009). Ed. *The Oxford Handbook of Early Modern Theatre*, Oxford: Oxford University Press.

Dutton, Richard. (2016). *Shakespeare, Court Dramatist*, Oxford: Oxford University Press.

Egan, Gabriel. (2011). Precision, Consistency, and Completeness in Early-Modern Playbook Manuscripts: The Evidence from *Thomas of Woodstock* and *John a Kent and John a Cumber*. *The Library* 12:4, 376–91.

Erne, Lukas. (2003). *Shakespeare as Literary Dramatist*, Cambridge: Cambridge University Press.

Finkelpearl, Philip J. (1966). John Marston's *Histrio-Mastix* as an Inns of Court Play: A Hypothesis. *Huntington Library Quarterly* 29, 223–34.

Fitzpatrick, Tim. (2011). *Playwright, Space, and Place in Early Modern Performance: Shakespeare and Company*, Farnham: Ashgate.

Foakes, R. A. (1985). *Illustrations of the English Stage, 1580–1642*, London: Scolar Press.

Foakes, R. A. (2002). Ed. *Henslowe's Diary*, Cambridge: Cambridge University Press.

Fotheringham, Richard. (2021). Staging Music in Shakespeare. *Australian Drama Studies* 78, 7–33.

Graves, R. B. (1999). *Lighting the Shakespearean Stage, 1567–1642*, Carbondale and Edwardsville: Southern Illinois University Press.

Graves, R. B. (2009). Lighting. In Richard Dutton, ed., *The Oxford Handbook of Early Modern Theatre*, Oxford: Oxford University Press, 528–42.

Greg, W. W. (1931). *Dramatic Documents from the Elizabethan Playhouses: Stage Plots, Actors' Parts, Prompt Books.* 2 Vols., Oxford: Clarendon Press.

Greg, W. W. (1939–1959). *A Bibliography of the English Printed Drama to the Restoration.* 4 Vols., London: Printed for the Bibliographical Society at the Oxford University Press.

Greg, W. W. (1955). *The Shakespeare First Folio: Its Bibliographical and Textual History*, Oxford: Clarendon Press.

Gurr, Andrew. (1989). The Tempest's Tempest at Blackfriars. *Shakespeare Survey* 41, 91–102.

Gurr, Andrew. (1996). *The Shakespearian Playing Companies*, Oxford: Oxford University Press.

Gurr, Andrew. (1999). Maximal and Minimal Texts: Shakespeare v. The Globe. *Shakespeare Survey* 52, 68–87.

Gurr, Andrew. (2004). *Playgoing in Shakespeare's London* 3rd ed., Cambridge: Cambridge University Press.

Gurr, Andrew and Mariko Ichikawa. (2000). *Staging in Shakespeare's Theatres*, Oxford: Oxford University Press.

Gurr, Andrew and Farah Karim-Cooper. (2014). Eds. *Moving Shakespeare Indoors: Performance and Repertoire in the Jacobean Playhouse*, Cambridge: Cambridge University Press.

Hammond, Anthony. (1992). Encounters of the Third Kind in Stage-Directions in Elizabethan and Jacobean Drama. *Studies in Philology* 89:1, 71–99.

Harbage, Alfred. (1964). *Annals of English Drama, 975–1700* rev. Samuel Schoenbaum, London: Methuen.

Hirrel, Michael J. (2010). Duration of Performances and Lengths of Plays: How Shall We Beguile the Lazy Time? *Shakespeare Quarterly* 61:2, 159–82.

Hirsh, James. (2002). Act Divisions in the Shakespeare First Folio. *Publications of the Bibliographical Society of America* 96:2, 219–56.

Holland, Peter. (2001). Beginning in the Middle. *Proceedings of the British Academy 111 2000 Lectures and Memoirs*, Oxford: Oxford University Press.

Hosley, Richard. (1966). Was there a Music-Room in Shakespeare's Globe? *Shakespeare Survey* 13, 113–23.

Hutchings, Mark. (2011). De Flores between the Acts. *Studies in Theatre & Performance* 33:1, 95–111.

Hutchings, Mark. (2013). The Interval and Indoor Playmaking. *Studies in Theatre & Performance* 33:3, 263–79.

Hutchings, Mark. (2023). The Changeling by Design. In John D. Sanderson, ed., *400 Años de The Changeling*, Alicante: Universitat d'Alacant, 37–55.

Ichikawa, Mariko. (2002). *Shakespearean Entrances*, Basingstoke: Palgrave Macmillan.

Ichikawa, Mariko. (2012). *The Shakespearean Stage Space* 2nd ed., Cambridge: Cambridge University Press.

Jackson, MacD. P. (2001). Shakespeare's *Richard II* and the Anonymous Thomas of Woodstock. *Medieval and Renaissance Drama in England* 14, 17–65.

Jewkes, Wilfred T. (1958). *Act Division in Elizabethan and Jacobean Plays, 1583–1616*, New York: AMS Press.

Johnson, Laurie. (2018). *Shakespeare's Lost Playhouse: Eleven Days at Newington Butts*, New York: Routledge.

Jonson, Ben. (1631). *The New Inn*. London

Jones, Emrys. (1971). *Scenic Form in Shakespeare*, Oxford: Clarendon Press.

Jonson, Ben. (1616). *The Workes of Beniamin Ionson*, London.

Jonson, Ben. (1988). *The Staple of News*. Ed. Anthony Parr, Manchester: Manchester University Press.

Jonson, Ben. (2000). *The Magnetic Lady*. Ed. Peter Happé, Manchester: Manchester University Press.

Kathman, David. (2004). Reconsidering 'The Seven Deadly Sins'. *Early Theatre* 7:1, 13–44.

Kathman, David. (2009). Inn-Yard Playhouses. In Richard Dutton, ed., *The Oxford Handbook of Early Modern Theatre*, Oxford: Oxford University Press, 153–67.

Kidnie, Margaret Jane. (2004). The Staging of Shakespeare's Drama in Print Editions. In Lukas Erne and Margaret Jane Kidnie, eds., *Textual Performances: The Modern Reproduction of Shakespeare's Drama*, Cambridge: Cambridge University Press, 158–77.

Kiernan, Pauline. (1999). *Staging Shakespeare at the New Globe*, Basingstoke: Macmillan.

Knutson, Roslyn L. (2002). Two Playhouses, Both Alike in Dignity. *Shakespeare Studies* 30, 111–17.

Knutson, Roslyn L. (2006). What If There Wasn't a 'Blackfriars Repertory'? In Paul Menzer, ed., *Inside Shakespeare: Essays on the Blackfriars Stage*, Selinsgrove: Susquehanna University Press, 54–60.

Kuhn, Thomas. (1996). *The Structure of Scientific Revolutions* 3rd ed., Chicago: University of Chicago Press.

Lawson, Mark. (2016). Pause and Effect: Tradition of Multiple Intervals Gets a Revival. *The Guardian*, 27 February. www.theguardian.com/stage/2016/feb/27/multiple-intervals-chekhov-ibsen.

Lindley, David. (2009). Blackfriars, Music and Masque: Theatrical Contexts of the Last Plays. In Catherine M. S. Alexander, ed., *The Cambridge Companion to Shakespeare's Last Plays*, Cambridge: Cambridge University Press, 29–45.

Long, William B. (1985). 'A Bed/for Woodstock': A Warning for the Unwary. *Medieval and Renaissance Drama in England* 2, 91–118.

Long, William B. (1999). 'Precious Few': English Manuscript Playbooks. In David Scott Kastan, ed., *A Companion to Shakespeare*, Oxford: Blackwell, 414–33.

Marston, John. (1975). *The Malcontent.* Ed. George K. Hunter, London: Methuen.

Marston, John. (1986). *Sophonisba*, in *Three Jacobean Witchcraft Plays*. Eds. Peter Corbin and Douglas Sedge, Manchester: Manchester University Press.

Massai, Sonia. (2004). Scholarly Editing and the Shift from Print to Electronic Cultures. In Lukas Erne and Margaret Jane Kidnie, eds., *Textual Performances: The Modern Reproduction of Shakespeare's Drama*, Cambridge: Cambridge University Press, 94–108.

May, Thomas. (1657). *The Life of a Satyrical Puppy Called Nim.* London

McMillin, Scott. (1973). The Plots of *The Dead Man's Fortune* and *The Seven Deadly Sins:* Inferences for Theatre Historians. *Studies in Bibliography* 26, 235–43.

Mehl, Dieter. (1965). *The Elizabethan Dumb Show: The History of a Dramatic Convention*, London: Methuen.

Menzer, Paul. (2006). Ed. *Inside Shakespeare: Essays on the Blackfriars Stage*, Selinsgrove: Susquehanna University Press.

Menzer, Paul. (2013). Lines. In Henry S. Turner, ed., *Early Modern Theatricality*, Oxford: Oxford University Press, 113–32.

Middleton, Thomas. (2007a). *The Phoenix*, eds., Lawrence Danson and Ivo Kamps. In Gary Taylor and John Lavagnino, gen. eds., *Thomas Middleton: The Collected Works*, Oxford: Oxford University Press, 91–127.

Middleton, Thomas. (2007b). *Your Five Gallants*, eds., Ralph Alan Cohen with John Jowett. In Gary Taylor and John Lavagnino, gen. eds., *Thomas Middleton: The Collected Works*, Oxford: Oxford University Press, 594–636.

Mowat, Barbara. (2001). The Reproduction of Shakespeare's Texts. In Margreta de Grazia and Stanley Wells, eds., *The Cambridge Companion to Shakespeare*, Cambridge: Cambridge University Press, 13–29.

Munro, Lucy. (2005). *Children of the Queen's Revels: A Jacobean Theatre Repertory*, Cambridge: Cambridge University Press.

Munro, Lucy. (2009). Music and Sound. In Richard Dutton, ed., *The Oxford Handbook of Early Modern Theatre*, Oxford: Oxford University Press, 543–59.

Munro, Lucy. (2020). *Shakespeare in the Theatre: The King's Men*, London: Bloomsbury.

Nelson, Alan H. (1989). *Cambridge* 2 Vols. Records of Early English Drama, Toronto: University of Toronto Press.

Nelson, Alan H. (1994). *Early Cambridge Theatres: College, University, and Town Stages, 1464–1720*, Cambridge: Cambridge University Press.

Newdigate, John. (2012). *The Humorous Magistrate*. Ed. Margaret Jane Kidnie, Manchester: Manchester University Press, for the Malone Society.

Oxford English Dictionary. (Oxford: Oxford University Press, 2010). Web.

Shakespeare, William. (1623). *Mr. William Shakespeares Comedies, Histories & Tragedies*, London.

Shakespeare, William. (1995). *Titus Andronicus*. Ed. Jonathan Bate, London: Routledge.

Shakespeare, William. (1997). *Titus Andronicus*. Ed. Katherine Eiseman Maus. In Stephen Greenblatt, gen., ed., *The Norton Shakespeare: Based on the Oxford Edition*, New York: W. W. Norton.

Shakespeare, William. (1999). The Tempest. Ed. Virginia Mason Vaughan and Alden T. Vaughan, Walton-on-Thames, Thomas Nelson.

Shakespeare, William. (2006). *Titus Andronicus*. Ed. Alan Hughes, Cambridge: Cambridge University Press.

Shirley, James. (1652). *The Doubtful Heir*. London

Smith, Irwin. (1964). *Shakespeare's Blackfriars Playhouse: Its History and Its Design*, New York: New York University Press.

Smith, Irwin. (1967). Their Exits and Reentrances. *Shakespeare Quarterly* 18:1, 7–16.

Smith, Joshua S. (2012). Reading between the Acts: Satire and the Interludes in *The Knight of the Burning Pestle. Studies in Philology* 109:4, 474–95.

Smith, Simon. The Many Performance Spaces for Music at Jacobean Indoor Playhouses. In Bill Barclay and David Lindley, eds., *Shakespeare, Music and Performance*, Cambridge: Cambridge University Press, 29–41.

Snuggs, Henry L. (1960). *Shakespeare and Five Acts: Studies in a Dramatic Convention*, New York: Vantage Press.

Somerset, Alan. (1994). 'How Chances It They Travel?': Provincial Touring, Playing Spaces, and the King's Men. *Shakespeare Survey* 47, 45–60.

Stern, Tiffany. (2009). *Documents of Performance in Early Modern England*, Cambridge: Cambridge University Press.

Stern, Tiffany. (2014). 'A Ruinous Monastery': The Second Blackfriars Playhouse as a Place of Nostalgia. In Andrew Gurr and Farah Karim-Cooper, eds., *Moving Shakespeare Indoors: Performance and Repertoire in the Jacobean Playhouse*, 97–114.

Stern, Tiffany. (2018). Inventing Stage Directions; Demoting Dumb Shows. In Sarah Dustagheer and Gillian Woods, eds., *Stage Directions and Shakespearean Theatre*, London: Bloomsbury, 19–43.

Streitberger, William. (2016). *The Masters of the Revels and Elizabeth I's Court Theatre*, Oxford: Oxford University Press.

Syme, Holger Schott. (2008). Unediting the Margin: Jonson, Marston, and the Theatrical Page. *English Literary Renaissance* 38:1, 142–71.

Syme, Holger Schott. (2018). Pastiche or Archetype? The Sam Wanamaker Playhouse and the Project of Theatrical Reconstruction. *Shakespeare Survey* 71, 135–46.

Taylor, Gary. (1979). Three Studies in the Text of *Henry V*. In Stanley Wells and Gary Taylor, *Modernizing Shakespeare's Spelling, with Three Studies in the Text of 'Henry V'*, Oxford: Clarendon Press, 37–164.

Taylor, Gary. (1993). The Structure of Performance: Act-Intervals in the London Theatres, 1576–1642. In Gary Taylor and John Jowett, eds., *Shakespeare Reshaped 1606–1623*, Oxford: Clarendon Press, 3–50.

Taylor, Gary, and John Lavagnino. (2007a). Gen. eds., *Thomas Middleton: The Collected Works*, Oxford: Oxford University Press.

Taylor, Gary, and John Lavagnino (2007b). Gen. eds., *Thomas Middleton and Early Modern Textual Culture*, Oxford: Oxford University Press.

Taylor, Gary, and Doug Duhaime. (2017). Who Wrote the Fly Scene (3.2) in *Titus Andronicus?* Automated Searches and Deep Reading. In Gary Taylor and Gabriel Egan, eds., *The New Oxford Shakespeare: Authorship Companion*, Oxford: Oxford University Press, 67–91.

Thomson, Leslie. (1996). A Quarto 'Marked for Performance': Evidence of What? *Medieval and Renaissance Drama in England* 8, 176–210.

Thomson, Leslie. (2010). Playgoers on the Outdoor Stages of Early Modern London. *Theatre Notebook* 14:1, 3–11.

Thomson, Leslie. (2013). Blackfriars Stage Sitters and the Staging of *The Tempest*, *The Maid's Tragedy*, and *The Two Noble Kinsmen*. In Kathryn M. Moncrief, Kathryn R. McPherson, and Sarah Enloe, eds., *Shakespeare Expressed: Page, Stage, and Classroom in Shakespeare and His Contemporaries*, Madison: Fairleigh Dickinson University Press, 175–85.

Thomson, Leslie. (2016). Dumb Shows in Performance on the Early Modern Stage. *Medieval and Renaissance Drama in England* 21, 17–45.

Tosh, Will. (2018). *Playing Indoors: Staging Early Modern Drama in the Sam Wanamaker Playhouse*, London: Bloomsbury.

Turner, Henry S. (2006). *The English Renaissance Stage: Geometry, Poetics, and the Practical Spatial Arts, 1580–1630*, Oxford: Oxford University Press.

Van Kampen, Claire. (2017). 'Music Still': Understanding and Reconstructing Shakespeare's Use of Musical Underscore. *Shakespeare Survey* 70, 30–39.

Wells, Stanley. *Re-editing Shakespeare for the Modern Reader*, Oxford: Clarendon Press.

Wells, Stanley and Gary Taylor. *Modernizing Shakespeare's Spelling, with Three Studies in the Text of 'Henry V'*, Oxford: Oxford University Press.

White, Martin. (1998). *Renaissance Drama in Action: An Introduction to Aspects of Theatre Practice and Performance*, London: Routledge.

White, Martin. (2014). 'When Torchlight Made an Artificial Noon': Light and Darkness in the Indoor Jacobean Theatre. In Andrew Gurr and Karim Karim-Cooper, eds., *Moving Shakespeare Indoors: Performance and Repertoire in the Jacobean Playhouse*, Cambridge: Cambridge University Press, 115–36.

White, Martin. (2018). 'By Indirections Find Directions Out': Unpicking Early Modern Stage Directions. In Sarah Dustagheer and Gillian Woods, eds., *Stage Directions and Shakespearean Theatre*, London: Bloomsbury, 191–211.

Womack, Peter. (2013). Off-Stage. In Henry S. Turner, ed., *Early Modern Theatricality*, Oxford: Oxford University Press, 71–92.

Womack, Peter. (2019). Embodied Theatre in *The Changeling*. In Mark Hutchings, ed., *'The Changeling': A Critical Reader*, London: Bloomsbury, 93–119.

Acknowledgements

This research was carried out as part of a project (Grant PID2020-113516GB-100), funded by Spain's Ministerio de Ciencia e Innovación and Agencia Estatal de Investigación. I would also like to thank the Spanish government for the award of a Beatriz Galindo (Senior) fellowship.

In memory, A. A. Bromham

A Note on the Texts and Abbreviations

Unless stated otherwise, all references to dramatic texts are to EEBO (Early English Books Online), except quotations from the Shakespeare First Folio, which are keyed to Charlton Hinman's facsimile edition (New York & London: W. W. Norton & Company, 1968; revised edn. ed. Peter W. M. Blayney, 1996). Throughout I use 'sd(s)' for stage direction(s), and act-breaks, for example, between acts 2 and 3, are signalled thus: '2/3'.

Cambridge Elements ☰

Shakespeare Performance

W. B. Worthen
Barnard College

W. B. Worthen is Alice Brady Pels Professor in the Arts, and Chair of the Theatre Department at Barnard College. He is also co-chair of the Ph.D. Program in Theatre at Columbia University, where he is Professor of English and Comparative Literature.

Cambridge Elements ☰

Shakespeare Performance

ELEMENTS IN THE SERIES

Shakespearean Futures: Casting the Bodies of Tomorrow on Shakespeare's Stages Today
Amy Cook

Robert Lepage's Intercultural Encounters
Christie Carson

A Short History of Shakespeare in Performance: From the Restoration to the Twenty-First Century
Richard Schoch

Viral Shakespeare: Performance in the Time of Pandemic
Pascale Aebischer

This Distracted Globe: Attending to Distraction in Shakespeare's Theatre
Jennifer J. Edwards

Shakespeare without Print
Paul Menzer

Shakespeare's Visionary Women
Laura Jayne Wright

Early Modern Media Ecology
Peter W. Marx

Sleep No More and the Discourses of Shakespeare Performance
D. J. Hopkins

Staging Disgust: Rape, Shame, and Performance in Shakespeare and Middleton
Jennifer Panek

Extended Reality Shakespeare
Aneta Mancewicz

Approaching the Interval in the Early Modern Theatre: The Significance of the 'Act-Time'
Mark Hutchings

A full series listing is available at: www.cambridge.org/ESPF

Printed in the United States
by Baker & Taylor Publisher Services